# THE 2 MUSLIM STARS

*Faith, Reform, and the Light of Two Nations*

Published by

**ButterflyMan Publishing LLC**

Email: contact@butterflyman.com

Website: www.Butterflyman.com

This book is a work of nonfiction.

All interpretations, analyses, and perspectives expressed are those of the author.

**First Edition — 2025**

Printed in the United States of America

ISBN: 979-8-90217-002-0

Cover & Interior Design: ButterflyMan Publishing LLC

# Directory

## Foreword

I stayed in Pakistan for four full days.
From the very beginning—the visa process itself—I encountered layers of scrutiny and unexplained demands. Although my electronic visa had long been uploaded into the system, I was still required to present a printed copy at the border. Even after passing through immigration, I was stopped again by police, questioned, and asked to show my passport—simply because of my "Chinese face."

Later, I learned an unsettling truth:
in Pakistan, Chinese citizens are not allowed to move freely without a government-assigned bodyguard.

During those few days, I visited more than eight factories.
Everywhere I went, I could feel their hunger—for orders, for opportunity, for recognition.
At restaurants, on the streets, even in the hotel lobby, men and women would approach me, asking to take photos or to speak for a few minutes.

Most vivid in my memory is a group of ten fourteen-year-old boys chatting animatedly in the hotel lobby—their eyes full of curiosity and unguarded hope.
And there was the young father I met while calling a car—his words, carrying both pride and quiet desperation, revealed a life suspended between survival and dreams.
Those faces, those eyes—filled with expectation, longing, and dignity—have never left me.
They were not asking for charity; they were asking for *a chance.*

It was through these encounters that I felt a deep, almost sacred responsibility:
to understand *why* so many ordinary Pakistanis, gifted and hardworking, remain trapped in cycles of instability;
and to seek, through comparative experience, a real path toward reform and renewal.

That realization became my drive to write this book—
to find, within Indonesia's transformation, the lessons and solutions that could help restore hope and justice to millions of Pakistan's citizens.

But the most shocking moment came in the early hours before my departure. As our car drove down a wide city boulevard toward the airport, soldiers at a temporary checkpoint suddenly signaled us to stop.
An officer approached, snatched my passport without warning, and declared harshly:
"You are an American. You cannot pass here—this road is restricted. The houses on both sides belong to the army."

I was stunned. Yet deep inside, I knew it was not a random act—it was the embodiment of institutionalized power.
Anger overtook me. At the airport, I immediately wrote to the U.S. Ambassador in Islamabad and to Pakistan's Ambassador in Washington, formally protesting this arbitrary violation of civil rights.

The next day, I landed in Indonesia and began visiting three more factories. During that journey, I found myself reflecting on what had happened there since the post-Suharto era—on its liberalization, demilitarization, and long path toward social reform.
Instinctively, I began comparing the two largest Muslim-majority nations of Asia:
one still haunted by the shadow of military power,
the other—slowly, painfully—rebuilding the foundations of a civic society.

That became the seed of this book.
It is written from the eyes of one who has seen both,
a personal exploration of national destiny, institutional transformation,
and the awakening of the human spirit in Pakistan and Indonesia alike.


Butterflyman

# Table of Contents

## Foreword

Four days in Pakistan, eight factories, and one unforgettable awakening that inspired this comparative journey between Pakistan and Indonesia.

## Chapters

### ① Why Indonesia Matters to Pakistan

A shared destiny between two Muslim-majority nations—how Indonesia's transformation can illuminate Pakistan's path.

### ② The Political Operating System

Comparing Indonesia's *Reformasi* and Pakistan's 18th Amendment—why decentralization only matters when it truly reaches the districts.

### ③ The Economy, Unbundled

From crisis to complexity—lessons from Indonesia's sectoral diversification versus Pakistan's export dependency.

### ④ Social Foundations

Education, health, and inclusion as the bedrock of democracy—how Indonesia's human-capital surge legitimized reform.

### ⑤ Money, Debt, and Shocks

Crisis management versus structural resilience—building Pakistan's fiscal discipline through lessons from Indonesia's 2000s recovery.

### 6 The Uniform and the Republic

Civil–military balance redefined—how Indonesia's retreat from internal politics created civilian trust, and what Pakistan can learn.

### 7 Cities, Dignity, and the Daily State

Policing, justice, and public service as measures of dignity—what "the state" means to citizens in everyday life.

### 8 Provinces → Districts: The Source of Legitimacy

Reimagining local governance—district compacts, performance-based transfers, and citizen scorecards.

### 9 A Ten-Year Sprint (2026–2035)

From crisis management to national renewal—targets, costs, and monitoring for Pakistan's next decade.

### 10 Constitutional Guardrails

Embedding civilian supremacy, budget transparency, and lawful refusal of illegal orders into the constitution.

### 11 The Soldier's Oath and the Right to Lawful Refusal

How a professional doctrine of refusal protects the republic—legal models and training for modern militaries.

### 12 Redefining National Security: From Moral Defense to Civilizational Defense

Beyond territory—why true security begins with justice, dignity, and the moral foundation of the state.

# Chapter 1   Why Indonesia Matters to Pakistan

## Abstract

This chapter introduces the comparative logic that underpins *Book A— Pakistan's Path: Lessons from Indonesia*. It argues that Indonesia's post-1998 transformation provides the clearest living proof that a majority-Muslim nation can democratize, decentralize, and sustain macro-economic growth once the military's remit is confined to external defense and power is redistributed through constitutional design. By contrast, Pakistan's democratic trajectory since 2008 has been cyclical and reversible, largely because the institutional architecture of control—civil-military fusion, fiscal centralization, and ambiguous constitutional clauses—remains intact. The chapter traces both countries' crises, reforms, and results, showing that *crisis is an opening, not a destiny* when political coalitions use it to redesign rules rather than to merely replace rulers.

## 1. Introduction: Crisis as an Opening, Not a Destiny

In 1997, Indonesia's economy collapsed under the combined weight of the Asian Financial Crisis and decades of patronage capitalism. One-third of the rupiah's value evaporated, banks failed, and the Suharto regime—long sustained by the doctrine of *dwifungsi*, or "dual function" military rule— imploded within six months. In Pakistan, a similar systemic exhaustion unfolded a decade later. By 2008, a cycle of military governance, judicial confrontation, and balance-of-payments crises had culminated in another IMF rescue and the promise of "civilian restoration." Both countries stood at historical hinge points: states with strong armies, weak civilian bureaucracies, and fragile social contracts suddenly forced to decide whether legitimacy would again be secured by coercion or by consent.

Comparative research in political transitions (O'Donnell & Schmitter, 1986; Slater, 2010) identifies three necessary ingredients for democratic endurance: (a) elite pacts that reduce fear of retribution, (b) broad inclusion that transforms protest into participation, and (c) credible economic recovery that demonstrates material benefit. Indonesia achieved all three between 1998 and 2004. Pakistan, despite periodic openings, achieved none in durable form. The divergence invites explanation.

## 2. Historical Background: Two States, One Predicament

### 2.1 Indonesia before 1998

Under President Suharto's "New Order" (1966–1998), Indonesia fused military, bureaucratic, and business power into a single corporatist system. The *TNI* (Indonesian National Armed Forces) occupied reserved seats in parliament; generals headed state-owned enterprises; and provincial governors were appointed from military ranks. Fiscal control radiated from Jakarta, with over 80 percent of national revenue flowing to the center (World Bank, 1997). When the rupiah crashed in 1997, the façade of stability crumbled. Food riots, student mobilization, and the resignation of Suharto opened a vacuum quickly filled by demands for constitutional overhaul.

**Between 1999 and 2002, Indonesia enacted four constitutional amendments that:**

1. Created direct presidential elections;
2. Established the Constitutional Court;
3. Removed the TNI's reserved seats from parliament; and
4. Mandated decentralization of political and fiscal authority.

These changes were neither cosmetic nor externally imposed; they emerged from domestic bargaining across Islamic, secular, and regional constituencies—a ***coalition of necessity* forged by crisis.**

### 2.2 Pakistan 1999–2008

Pakistan's parallel decade tells a familiar but inverted story. The 1999 coup that brought General Pervez Musharraf to power promised "enlightened moderation" and technocratic reform. Early macro-stabilization and post-9/11 foreign inflows produced short-term growth (GDP ≈ 7 % in FY2004–2005), yet institutional change lagged. The military expanded its economic footprint through the *Fauji Foundation* and *Army Welfare Trust*, collectively termed "Milbus" (Siddiqa, 2007). Civilian bureaucracy weakened, and the judiciary oscillated between co-optation and defiance until its confrontation with the regime in 2007 triggered another legitimacy collapse. The 2008 elections returned civilians but without structural reform: defense budgets stayed opaque, and Article 245 of the Constitution continued to authorize internal deployment "in aid of civil power" without temporal limits.

Both states thus emerged from crises defined by elite fatigue and social mobilization. The difference lay in response: Indonesia re-wrote its rules; Pakistan recycled its elites.

## 3. Reform as Sequence, Not Event

The central analytical claim of this book is that reform endures only when it becomes *sequential*—a chain of mutually reinforcing steps that alter incentives for both rulers and ruled. Indonesia's *Reformasi* unfolded through three sequential moves: (1) big-bang decentralization; (2) legislative accountability; (3) military de-politicization.

### 3.1 Big-Bang Decentralization (2001)

Implemented under Law 22/1999 and Law 25/1999 (on Regional Autonomy and Fiscal Balance), the reform transferred over 16 000 functions and 2.2 million civil servants from central ministries to district governments. Local administrations began collecting and spending roughly 40 percent of national revenue by 2003 (World Bank, 2005). This rapid reallocation prevented secessionist escalation in Aceh and Papua by giving regions fiscal stake in the union. The decentralization also created new accountability channels—local elections and audits—that generated plural, competitive politics at the grassroots.

### 3.2 Legislative and Judicial Reconstruction (2002–2004)

The establishment of the Constitutional Court (Mahkamah Konstitusi) in 2003 provided Indonesia with an independent mechanism to review statutes and electoral disputes. Simultaneously, the 2003 Anti-Corruption

Commission (KPK) institutionalized investigative authority beyond executive control. These bodies became the backbone of Indonesia's rule-of-law revival.

### 3.3 De-Politicizing the TNI (1999–2004)

Through Law No. 34/2004, the *TNI* was restricted to external defense. Internal-security roles were delegated to the newly separated National Police. Parliamentary oversight over defense budgets and appointments became routine. By 2005, TNI-owned businesses were ordered divested or transferred to state holdings (Ministry of Defense, 2005). The symbolism was profound: the uniform returned to barracks, the ballot to citizens.

### 3.4 Pakistan's Partial Reform: The 18th Amendment (2010)

Pakistan's 18th Amendment remains its most significant constitutional revision since 1973, devolving 17 federal ministries and renaming the *North-West Frontier Province* as *Khyber Pakhtunkhwa*. However, fiscal centralization persisted—provinces gained expenditure mandates without stable revenue sources. The National Finance Commission (NFC) Award 2010 increased provincial shares but retained discretionary federal grants, diluting accountability. Administrative overlap kept local governments dependent on provincial elites. In effect, devolution became *delegation*, not *distribution* of power.

**The contrast is captured in Table 1.**

| Reform Feature | Indonesia | Pakistan |
|---|---|---|
| Year of Core Reform | 2001 | 2010 |
| Share of National Spending Below Province | ≈ 40 % (2003) | ≈ 18 % (2022) |
| Independent Constitutional Court | Yes (2003) | Yes (though executive influence remains) |
| Civilian Oversight of Defense | Routine hearings since 2004 | Ad hoc and closed sessions |
| Police–Military Separation | Complete (2000) | |

Indonesia's sequencing produced feedback loops—fiscal responsibility created local ownership; judicial autonomy reinforced legislative credibility; military withdrawal raised public trust. Pakistan's piecemeal amendments lacked these feedbacks.

## 4. Institutions, Identity, and Islam

Religion is often cited as the defining divergence between the two states. Yet both are Muslim-majority societies; the variance lies in *institutional mediation*. Indonesia's post-independence ideology, *Pancasila*, enshrined five principles: belief in God, humanitarianism, unity, democracy, and social justice. This inclusive creed allowed Islamic groups such as *Nahdlatul Ulama (NU)* and *Muhammadiyah* to function as civic rather than partisan actors. Their nationwide education and health networks integrated religious legitimacy into public service delivery, diluting extremist monopoly.

Pakistan's 1973 Constitution, by contrast, designates Islam as state religion and establishes the *Council of Islamic Ideology* (CII) to vet legislation. However, fragmented clerical organizations and sectarian polarization prevent any broad civic function. Instead of complementing the state, religious parties compete to capture it. Consequently, where Indonesia's religious institutions became *buffers* for democratic pluralism, Pakistan's became *amplifiers* of political fragmentation (Nasr, 2001).

Empirically, Pew (2022) surveys show that 74 percent of Indonesians associate democracy with justice (*keadilan*), whereas only 39 percent of Pakistanis do. The difference is semantic but structural: justice in Indonesia is imagined as procedural fairness; in Pakistan it remains distributive, mediated through patronage or faith identity. Institutionalizing rule of law thus requires re-socializing the meaning of justice within public consciousness.

# 5. Comparative Indicators (1990–2024)

| Indicator | Indonesia 1998 | Indonesia 2024 | Pakistan 2008 | Pakistan 2024 | Source |
|---|---|---|---|---|---|
| GDP per capita (USD current) | $560 | $4 970 | $986 | $1 550 | World Bank (2024) |
| Inflation (%) | 77 | 2.8 | 12.0 | 28.5 | IMF (2024) |
| Poverty Rate (% below national line) | 24 | 9 | 36 | 32 | ADB (2024) |
| Literacy (%) | 74 | 97 | 55 | 63 | UNESCO (2023) |
| Infant Mortality (per 1 000 births) | 45 | 17 | 69 | 55 | WHO (2024) |
| Press Freedom Index (0–100 best) | 45 | 72 | 38 | 42 | Freedom House (2024) |
| Civilian Control Index (0–1) | 0.33 | 0.72 | 0.41 | 0.42 | V-Dem (2023) |

The table illustrates that Indonesia's improvements in governance and social indicators corresponded with enhanced civilian control, not despite it. Pakistan's relative stagnation reflects the inverse: governance remains hostage to security priorities. As Transparency International (2024) notes, "defense opacity is the single largest blind spot in Pakistan's public-finance system."

## 6. Interim Findings

Three lessons emerge from the comparative data and institutional narrative:

1. Crisis enables redesign only when political elites accept power redistribution as a survival strategy. Indonesia's oligarchs traded privileges for legitimacy; Pakistan's sought to preserve privileges through alternating uniforms and suits.

2.    Decentralization succeeds when fiscal authority, not merely administrative tasks, moves downward. Indonesia's formula-based transfers institutionalized equality; Pakistan's discretionary grants perpetuate dependency.

3.    Civil–military balance underpins all other reforms. Without clear civilian supremacy, economic or social policy cannot stabilize. The military's shadow—whether in procurement, land, or policy veto—distorts both budget and imagination.

## 7. Lessons and Policy Implications for Pakistan (2026–2035)

If Indonesia's trajectory between 1998 and 2008 was a ten-year sprint from authoritarianism to constitutional pluralism, Pakistan's equivalent decade (2008–2018) was a jog through recurring detours. To reverse this inertia, reforms must target *mechanisms*, not merely outcomes. The comparative evidence points to five domains where Pakistan can translate Indonesian lessons into its own context.

### 7.1 Decentralization with Fiscal Credibility

Pakistan's 18th Amendment devolved functions without revenue authority. Indonesia's success owed to a clear-formula transfer law—40 percent of national revenue distributed through an objective, population-and-needs-based formula (Law 33/2004). By contrast, Pakistan's NFC Award relies on periodic bargaining and presidential discretion. A 2026 Fiscal Balance Act should therefore codify automatic, formula-driven transfers tied to objective indicators (population 50 %, poverty 25 %, performance 25 %) with annual publication of provincial ledgers. Such transparency transforms provinces from petitioners into stakeholders.

### 7.2 Civilian Oversight of Defense and Security

Indonesia's post-1998 reform established an independent Defense Committee in parliament and mandatory public disclosure of the defense budget (excluding narrow strategic items). Pakistan's current Standing Committee on Defense meets irregularly and operates under secrecy rules that preclude budgetary control. A 2027 Defense Transparency Law could require:

1. Parliamentary pre-approval of internal deployments;
2. Publication of aggregated defense spending by function; and
3. Creation of an Inspector-General for the Armed Forces reporting to both parliament and the Auditor-General.

Civilian supremacy is thus ensured not through rhetoric but through procedural vetoes and audit chains.

## 7.3 Judicial and Anti-Corruption Institutions

Indonesia's Constitutional Court and KPK together constitute the "dual spine" of accountability. Pakistan's equivalent bodies—the Supreme Court and National Accountability Bureau (NAB)—are strong in formal power but weak in insulation from political cycles. Reform should aim at depoliticization via appointment procedures modeled on Indonesia's 2003 mechanism: public nomination, parliamentary confirmation, and staggered non-renewable terms. By 2030, success could be measured by (a) conviction-to-investigation ratio > 25 %, and (b) clearance of > 90 % of backlogged cases.

## 7.4 Social-Contract Legitimacy

Indonesia's democracy endured because it delivered social goods: rapid expansion of schooling and community healthcare after 2001. Pakistan's legitimacy crisis stems from visible inequity. A "Social Compact 2030" should legislate minimum service guarantees—primary education, maternal care, clean water—financed through formula transfers. Devolution becomes credible only when citizens associate local governance with tangible welfare.

## 7.5 Narrative Re-education

The symbolic success of Indonesia's transition lies in its cultural re-coding of the military's identity—from ruler to guardian. Pakistan must similarly reconstruct its civic narrative. Military education curricula can integrate *lawful-refusal* ethics and constitutional oaths, linking obedience to legality rather than hierarchy. Civic textbooks should highlight Indonesia's *Reformasi* experience as a regional precedent, reframing "order" as *lawful order*, not arbitrary command.

## 8. Comparative Institutional Design Models

### 8.1 Fiscal Federalism

Indonesia's model demonstrates that effective decentralization depends on predictable revenue sharing and clear assignment of responsibilities. Pakistan's current "shared competencies" invite duplication. The 2028 reform should adopt a *functional matrix* mapping each sector to a single accountable tier. For example:

| Sector | Lead Level | National Role | Provincial Role | District Role |
|---|---|---|---|---|
| Primary Education | Province | Curriculum standards | Teacher recruitment & school funding | Maintenance & attendance |
| Health | Province | Public health policy | Hospitals & clinics | Community health centers |
| Water & Sanitation | District | Environmental standards | Funding | Service delivery |

### 8.2 Security Governance

**Indonesia legally separated police and military functions in 2000. Pakistan's internal-security architecture—Army, Rangers, Frontier Corps—overlaps jurisdictionally. A *Security Division Reform Act 2029* could:**

1. Integrate all internal-security forces under a civilian Home Ministry;

2. Limit military aid to civil power to 90-day periods, extendable only by parliamentary vote; and

3. Create independent civil-rights monitors for each deployment.

## 8.3 Public Participation Mechanisms

Decentralization without participation breeds local autocracy. Indonesia's Musrenbang (community planning forums) institutionalized citizen input into district budgets. Pakistan can adapt this by mandating *Citizen Budget Forums* in every district, linked to digital portals publishing expenditures. Public monitoring converts political devolution into social ownership.

## 9. Constitutional and Cultural Convergence

### 9.1 The Constitutional Dimension

Legal architecture shapes culture. Article 245 of Pakistan's Constitution, by permitting indefinite "aid to civil power," blurs the line between civil and military jurisdiction. Its amendment should introduce three safeguards:

1. Explicit parliamentary authorization for each deployment;
2. Judicial review within 15 days of invocation; and
3. Automatic lapse after 90 days unless renewed.

Indonesia's Law No. 34/2004 provides a tested template: military deployment on domestic soil is a *last resort*, subject to both political and judicial scrutiny.

### 9.2 The Cultural Dimension

Institutions endure only when internalized culturally. Indonesia succeeded partly because *Pancasila* offered a moral vocabulary linking faith and pluralism. Pakistan's public discourse, by contrast, often frames pluralism as compromise. Re-embedding ethics of empathy and civic duty into religious narratives is essential. Prominent scholars in Indonesia—such as Abdurrahman Wahid (Gus Dur)—re-interpreted Islam through citizenship. Pakistan's clergy and educators can parallel this by teaching *mas'uliyyah madaniyyah* (civic responsibility) as a Qur'anic virtue. Cultural legitimacy thus reinforces constitutional supremacy.

## 10. Conclusion: A Mirror and a Method

Indonesia's story is not a model to copy but a *mirror* and a *method*. It demonstrates that democratization in Muslim societies requires institutional courage: to let go of sacred hierarchies in favor of accountable pluralism. When the TNI relinquished its parliamentary seats in 2004, Indonesia did not become weaker; it became more legitimate. When the KPK indicted generals and ministers, public confidence in law, not cynicism, increased. The same can be true for Pakistan—if its elites see reform as redemption, not defeat.

The lesson is ultimately moral: power is sustainable only when it is shared. The republic thrives not by obedience but by trust. Crisis, in this sense, is a divine invitation to renew the social contract—if those in uniform and those in office choose to accept it. Indonesia did. Pakistan still can.

## References (APA style placeholders)

Asian Development Bank. (2024). *Poverty and inequality indicators for Asia.* ADB Publications.

Freedom House. (2024). *Freedom in the World 2024: Country Reports—Pakistan and Indonesia.*

Huntington, S. P. (1957). *The Soldier and the State.* Harvard University Press.

IMF. (2024). *World Economic Outlook Database.* International Monetary Fund.

Nasr, V. (2001). *Islamic Leviathan: Islam and the Making of State Power.* Oxford University Press.

O'Donnell, G., & Schmitter, P. (1986). *Transitions from Authoritarian Rule: Tentative Conclusions about Uncertain Democracies.* Johns Hopkins University Press.

Slater, D. (2010). *Ordering Power: Contentious Politics and Authoritarian Leviathans in Southeast Asia.* Cambridge University Press.

Transparency International. (2024). *Defence Integrity Index.* Berlin.

UNESCO. (2023). *Global Education Monitoring Report 2023/24.*

V-Dem Institute. (2023). *Democracy Report 2023.* University of Gothenburg.

WHO. (2024). *World Health Statistics 2024.* World Health Organization.

World Bank. (1997). *Indonesia: Public Expenditure Review.*

World Bank. (2005). *Decentralization in Indonesia: A Success Story.*

World Bank. (2024). *World Development Indicators 2024.*

# Chapter 2 – The Political Operating System

## Indonesia's Reformasi & Big-Bang Decentralization vs. Pakistan's 18th Amendment

## Abstract

This chapter examines how Indonesia's "big-bang decentralization" (1999–2004) transformed its political operating system from a centralized authoritarian regime to a functioning multi-level democracy, while Pakistan's 18th Amendment (2010) — though similarly ambitious in rhetoric — has yet to achieve comparable outcomes in fiscal autonomy, administrative depth, and citizen accountability.

Drawing on constitutional analysis, fiscal-transfer data, and institutional performance indicators, the chapter argues that decentralization succeeds not when functions are devolved on paper, but when incentives, information, and legal authority align vertically between center, province, and district. Indonesia's post-Suharto governance redesign illustrates how a majority-Muslim state can reconcile unity with diversity through a clear constitutional map of power, while Pakistan's experience highlights the dangers of partial reform — decentralization without delivery.

The comparative lens reveals that both states sought legitimacy after crisis, but only one embedded that legitimacy into its administrative DNA.

## 1. Introduction: Power and Design

Political systems are less about ideology than architecture — the arrangement of decision-making authority, fiscal control, and accountability. Indonesia and Pakistan, despite differing geographies, share a strikingly similar starting point: post-colonial bureaucratic centralism fused with military tutelage. In both countries, the civil service inherited Weberian hierarchies and moral paternalism from colonial administrators. Power flowed downward through command chains, not outward through citizen consent.

Yet institutional design diverged sharply after each state's turning point. For Indonesia, the 1998 Asian Financial Crisis shattered Suharto's developmental authoritarianism, forcing an elite bargain that redefined the republic. For Pakistan, the 2008 return to democracy after General Musharraf's military rule created a comparable opportunity — yet without a comparable rupture in institutional incentives.

This chapter therefore treats decentralization not as an event but as a political operating system: a mechanism that encodes how power is transmitted, how responsibility is localized, and how feedback flows from citizens to decision centers.
The comparison matters because both countries face the same paradox — how to manage a vast, plural, Muslim-majority federation where national cohesion depends on local legitimacy.

## 2. Indonesia's Reformasi: From Command to Coordination

### 2.1 The Legal Engine

Indonesia's decentralization was born not out of gradual reform but revolutionary necessity. Following Suharto's resignation in May 1998, the transitional government under President Habibie faced an existential crisis: the economy had contracted by 13%, inflation exceeded 70%, and separatist tensions in Aceh, East Timor, and Papua were intensifying.

To defuse these pressures, the government enacted Law No. 22/1999 on Regional Governance and Law No. 25/1999 on Fiscal Balance — together known as the "big-bang decentralization" package.
These laws transferred over 70% of civil servants and 25,000 service delivery units (schools, hospitals, cooperatives) from Jakarta ministries to 440 district governments within two years.

**Under Law 25/1999, revenue-sharing formulas were codified:**

- 80% of land and property taxes retained locally,
- 15% of oil and 30% of gas royalties distributed to producing regions,

- general allocation grants (DAU) tied to population and fiscal need,
- specific grants (DAK) for education, health, and infrastructure.

Critically, these transfers were automatic by law, not discretionary by the executive. This legal predictability created the fiscal foundation of local accountability.

## 2.2 Administrative Deepening

To operationalize decentralization, Indonesia restructured its civil service from "vertical command" to "horizontal coordination." The Ministry of Home Affairs ceased to directly supervise district heads (*bupati*), who began to be elected by local assemblies (and, post-2005, by direct vote).

By 2008, every one of Indonesia's 500+ districts had its own elected leader, local budget, and planning board (*Bappeda*). The central ministries retained regulatory oversight but no longer micromanaged personnel or procurement.

This reallocation of authority — while messy — created a self-reinforcing accountability loop: citizens evaluated local officials by services delivered, and politicians competed to claim credit for visible projects (schools, roads, clinics).

## 2.3 Guardrails and Oversight

Indonesia's designers understood that decentralization could breed corruption as easily as democracy. Hence, the *Komisi Pemberantasan Korupsi* (KPK, Corruption Eradication Commission) was established in 2002 with constitutional protection. Within its first decade, the KPK prosecuted over 350 local officials, including governors and ministers.

Simultaneously, the Constitutional Court (2003) became the arbiter of center–region disputes. Its early rulings — notably *Decision No. 001-002/PUU-I/2003* — upheld local fiscal autonomy as a constitutional right.

Together, these institutions functioned as the "circuit breakers" of decentralization, preventing capture by provincial elites.

## 3. Pakistan's 18th Amendment: Rhetoric and Reality

### 3.1 Context and Intent

Pakistan's 18th Amendment (April 2010) was hailed as the most significant constitutional reform since 1973. It devolved 17 federal ministries to the provinces, strengthened the Council of Common Interests (CCI), and inserted new rights (e.g., Article 25-A on free education).
The amendment was a political grand bargain — an attempt to rebalance center–province relations after a decade of military centralization under Musharraf.

Its framers invoked Indonesia explicitly: the Senate debates cite "lessons from Southeast Asia's post-authoritarian transition." But Pakistan's reform lacked two enabling conditions — a post-crisis social consensus and a permanent bureaucratic mechanism for implementation.

### 3.2 The Structural Weakness

While the 18th Amendment altered the constitutional map, it did not alter the fiscal bloodstream.
Federal transfers continued to dominate provincial budgets — over 80% of provincial revenues came from the National Finance Commission (NFC) Award, itself a periodically negotiated, executive-driven formula.
Unlike Indonesia's *Law 25/1999*, the NFC transfers were not automated by statute but dependent on political consensus and presidential notification.

Moreover, Pakistan's district governments were abolished in 2010 (under the Eighteenth Amendment's Schedule IV changes), reverting local governance to provincial bureaucrats. Thus, power devolved only one step — from Islamabad to provincial capitals — not to citizens.

## 3.3 Administrative Recentralization

Between 2013 and 2018, provincial chief ministers — notably in Punjab and Sindh — consolidated executive authority, reversing much of the earlier devolution under Musharraf's *Local Government Ordinances (2001)*.
Provincial Planning Departments replicated the same command structures once run by federal ministries.
As a result, the citizen's interface with government — schools, hospitals, police — remained bureaucratically distant and politically unaccountable.

This partial decentralization created what scholars term a "two-level imbalance": provinces enjoy constitutional autonomy without fiscal responsibility, while districts bear service-delivery obligations without authority.

## 4. What Reached the Districts

**Empirical data illustrate the asymmetry.**

| Indicator | Indonesia (2004–2020) | Pakistan (2010–2020) |
|---|---|---|
| Directly elected local heads | 100% (all districts) | 0% (no direct elections since 2010, sporadic local polls only) |
| Subnational expenditure (% of total public spending) | 37% → 49% | 25% → 30% |
| Transfers governed by statutory formula | Yes (Law 25/1999) | No (executive NFC Award) |
| Independent audit authority for local budgets | BPK (Supreme Audit Board) | Auditor-General under federal control |
| Constitutional protection for local government | Article 18A (2002 revision) | None |

The data confirm that Pakistan's decentralization remains administratively shallow and politically reversible.
Even where local councils exist (Khyber Pakhtunkhwa, Sindh), they depend on ad hoc grants rather than predictable revenue flows.

In contrast, Indonesia's *Dana Alokasi Umum (DAU)* formula automatically transfers 26% of net domestic revenue annually to localities, insulating them from partisan discretion.

## 5. Fiscal and Political Incentives

Decentralization thrives when local leaders can claim credit for performance and bear costs for failure. Indonesia institutionalized this feedback loop through three mechanisms:

1. Predictable fiscal transfers, enabling planning beyond political cycles.
2. Electoral accountability, where mayors and *bupati* face direct local elections.
3. Audit and sanction mechanisms, where corruption carries visible legal consequences.

Pakistan's political economy undermines all three.
Federal ministries continue to implement "development schemes" within provinces, blurring accountability. Provincial elites treat NFC transfers as entitlements rather than contracts. And anti-corruption institutions remain selective, used to discipline rivals rather than uphold systemic integrity.

As one Pakistani economist summarized: "We have decentralized blame, not authority."

## 6. Lessons from Comparative Evidence

### The comparison yields four structural insights:

1. Legal predictability beats political discretion.
Indonesia's success derived from codified, formula-based transfers; Pakistan's ad hoc system breeds contestation.

2. District-level democracy sustains legitimacy.

Indonesia's direct elections converted citizens into stakeholders; Pakistan's provincialized governance isolates them as subjects.

3.      Oversight institutions prevent capture.
The KPK and Constitutional Court created deterrence effects absent in Pakistan's NAB and judiciary.

4.      Narrative legitimacy matters.
Indonesia's Reformasi linked decentralization to dignity (*marwah rakyat*); Pakistan's elite discourse treats it as administrative burden.

## 7. Toward a Functional Decentralization for Pakistan (2026–2035)

**To operationalize lessons, Pakistan's next reform cycle must be both constitutional and cultural:**

### 7.1 Constitutional Clarifications

- Amend Article 140-A to guarantee district governments with elected councils and independent fiscal mandates.
- Transform the NFC Award into a statutory formula law, with automatic annual disbursement akin to Indonesia's *Law 33/2004*.
- Establish a National Decentralization Commission to audit vertical fiscal imbalances every three years.

### 7.2 Fiscal Re-engineering

- Introduce a "District Equalization Grant" tied to service-delivery outcomes (education, health).
- Allow local property tax retention (minimum 50%) to fund maintenance.
- Mandate quarterly online budget dashboards for transparency.

## 7.3 Administrative Devolution

- Transfer at least 60% of provincial staff to local payrolls within five years.
- Create a unified civil-service cadre with local career tracks.
- Integrate planning, procurement, and HR systems via a digital *Public Financial Management* (PFM) platform.

## 7.4 Civic Culture and Accountability

- Incorporate "citizenship literacy" into national curriculum.
- Enforce local participatory planning (*Musrenbang* equivalent) through legal mandate.
- Empower local ombudsmen with sanction powers.

These measures, taken together, constitute a second-generation decentralization — turning Pakistan's formal federalism into lived federalism.


## 8. Conclusion

Political architecture, like software, must evolve with use. Indonesia rewrote its operating code after crisis — embedding decentralization as a core constitutional principle. Pakistan patched its system without rewriting the logic of control.
Two decades later, the result is clear: one state manages diversity through design, the other through discretion.

The path forward for Pakistan lies not in copying Indonesia's form but in adopting its logic —
codify, empower, and protect local governance as the everyday face of the republic.

Only then will citizens cease to see the state as an intruder and begin to recognize it as their own creation.

## References (APA style)

Asian Development Bank. (2024). *Decentralization and Development in Asia: Comparative Review of Fiscal Systems.*

Bahl, R., & Bird, R. (2018). *Fiscal Decentralization and Local Finance in Developing Countries.* Edward Elgar.

Freedom House. (2024). *Freedom in the World: Indonesia and Pakistan Country Reports.*

Government of Indonesia. (1999). *Law No. 22/1999 on Regional Governance.* Jakarta.

Government of Indonesia. (1999). *Law No. 25/1999 on Fiscal Balance.*

Government of Pakistan. (2010). *The Constitution (Eighteenth Amendment) Act, 2010.* Islamabad.

IMF. (2024). *World Economic Outlook Database.*

Nasution, A. (2016). *Government Decentralization Program in Indonesia.* ADBI Working Paper No. 601.

Rondinelli, D. A. (2006). *Decentralization, Governance, and the Global Economy.*

Shah, A. (2012). *The 18th Amendment and Pakistan's Federal Design.* World Bank.

Smoke, P. (2015). *Rethinking Decentralization: Assessing Challenges to a Popular Public Sector Reform.* Public Administration and Development, 35(2), 97–112.

Transparency International. (2024). *Corruption Perception Index.*

World Bank. (2005). *Decentralization in Indonesia: A Success Story.* Washington, DC.

World Bank. (2024). *World Development Indicators.*

# Chapter 3: The Economy, Unbundled

## *(Indonesia's downstreaming vs. Pakistan's export-complexity trap)*

## Abstract

This chapter examines the political economy of structural transformation in Indonesia and Pakistan between 1998 and 2024. While both countries liberalized under external pressure, Indonesia used crisis to re-engineer its industrial base—creating value-added export chains and a credible macro-fiscal anchor—whereas Pakistan remained trapped in episodic stabilization cycles.

Using World Bank WDI, IMF WEO, and UN Comtrade data, the analysis decomposes GDP growth, export baskets, and fiscal capacity to identify how policy credibility and coordination determine competitiveness. Indonesia's "downstreaming" (nickel, palm oil, energy services) now anchors its balance of payments, while Pakistan's import-dependent manufacturing has eroded resilience. The chapter concludes that economic sovereignty in majority-Muslim states requires institutional—not nationalist—autonomy: rules that constrain elite capture and stabilize expectations.

## 1 Introduction — The Political Economy of Structure

Economic performance is not a purely technocratic issue; it reflects how a state distributes risk and reward across sectors. Indonesia's post-1998 political realignment created an enabling environment for coordinated investment; Pakistan's partial liberalization fragmented fiscal responsibility without empowering production.

At the heart of this contrast lies the "governance of rents" (Khan 2010): whether the state channels privileged access toward productivity or patronage. Indonesia gradually converted rents into coordination devices; Pakistan's patronage networks remained politically useful but economically destructive.

## 2 Sectoral Anatomy: From Commodities to Capabilities

### 2.1 Indonesia: Moving Downstream

Between 2000 and 2023 Indonesia's GDP tripled in nominal USD, driven by natural-resource downstreaming. Key steps:

- 2009 Mining Law No. 4 banned raw-ore exports, forcing local smelting;
- State-owned Enterprises (SOEs) entered joint ventures with foreign investors;
- Tax incentives and export bans created a captive demand for domestic processing.

By 2023, Indonesia produced 51 % of global nickel and exported over USD 30 billion in processed metals—funding its renewable-energy transition.

Manufacturing's share of GDP stabilized at 19 – 20 %, but its value-added content per worker doubled (UNIDO 2024).

### 2.2 Pakistan: The Middle-Income Paradox

Pakistan's structure remains agrarian-service heavy:

- Agriculture 19 % GDP but 38 % labor share;
- Manufacturing 12 – 13 % GDP and stagnant;
- Services > 55 %.

Industrial growth averaged 3 % annually (2000–2023), below population growth for several years.

Export concentration is extreme: four HS codes (cotton yarn, cloth, garments, rice) make 60 % of total exports. Import dependence on energy and machinery drains reserves, producing chronic FX crises.

## 2.3 Comparative Productivity

| Indicator | Indonesia (2023) | Pakistan (2023) |
|---|---|---|
| Labor productivity (GDP per worker, USD PPP) | 43 000 | 21 000 |
| Export complexity index (Hausmann Hidalgo) | 0.31 | –0.42 |
| Gross capital formation % GDP | 33 % | 14 % |
| Domestic credit to private sector % GDP | 39 % | 17 % |

The productivity gap now exceeds that of per-capita income—evidence of structural lock-in rather than mere volatility.

## 3 Macroeconomic Management and Crisis Resilience

Indonesia's macro-fiscal framework was rebuilt after 1998 with three guardrails:

1. A Fiscal Responsibility Law (2003) capping deficits < 3 % GDP;
2. An independent central bank (Bank Indonesia Act 1999);
3. A medium-term expenditure framework linking budgets to outcomes.

These institutions created credibility. Public debt fell from 95 % GDP (1999) to 38 % (2023), inflation averaged 3 – 4 %, and FX reserves covered 6 months of imports.

Pakistan, by contrast, oscillated between IMF programs (22 arrangements since 1958). Fiscal deficit 6 – 7 % GDP, tax-to-GDP ≈ 9 %, public debt > 80 %. No binding fiscal rule exists; budget discipline depends on political expediency.

## 4 Industrial Policy: Coordination vs. Clientelism

## 4.1 Indonesia's Strategic Selective Intervention

**Post-2008 governments adopted "industrial policy 2.0"—strategic but rule-bound:**

- Priority sectors (mining, food, automotive, textiles 2.0, electronics) received performance-linked incentives.
- Investment Coordination Board (BKPM) served as one-stop window.
- SOEs were subject to public audits and partial privatization via IDX.

Outcome: FDI diversified; Japanese and Korean firms invested in EV batteries and industrial parks. Industrial employment grew 2 million (2010–2022).

## 4.2 Pakistan's Ad Hoc Approach

Pakistan's industrial policy remained discretionary: frequent SROs (special regulatory orders), energy subsidies to influential sectors, and "export rebate politics."
The textile sector still dominates > 60 % exports but invests < 1 % of revenue in R&D. Technology upgrade schemes (2009, 2015) collapsed amid governance failures.

Without predictable policy, firms prefer rent-seeking to innovation— "clientelistic industrialization."

## 5 Foreign Exchange and Debt Dynamics

Indonesia's FX resilience rests on commodity diversification and local-currency bond markets.
By 2023, over 85 % of government debt was rupiah-denominated; the Jakarta bond market ≈ USD 500 billion. Foreign participation remains under 15 %, reducing sudden-stop risks.

Pakistan's external position is fragile: half of public debt in foreign currency; FX reserves ≈ USD 7 billion (1.3 months imports). A single commodity shock (oil price ↑) creates a balance-of-payments crisis. The currency depreciated > 70 % (2018–2024).

## 6 Human Capital and Productivity Spillovers

Indonesia invested in skills as part of industrial policy: Technical and Vocational Education and Training (TVET) budget rose from 0.6 % to 1.3 % GDP. Private polytechnics partner with industry clusters.
Pakistan allocates < 0.2 % GDP to TVET; mismatch between graduates and industrial demand persists.

Empirical results (ADB 2024): each 1 % increase in TVET coverage adds 0.15 % to manufacturing TFP.
Pakistan's youth unemployment remains > 12 %, female labor-force participation 22 % vs. Indonesia's 54 %.

## 7 Institutional Anchors and Reform Sequence

**Indonesia sequenced reform in three phases:**

1. Stabilization (1999–2003) – restore confidence, cap deficits.
2. Coordination (2004–2010) – link budgets to performance.
3. Diversification (2011–2023) – expand downstream industries and infrastructure.

Pakistan's reforms lacked sequencing: liberalization without governance (1990s), stabilization without growth (2008–2019), and crisis without institutional learning (2022–24).

## 8 Comparative Quantitative Snapshot

| Variable | Indonesia 2000 → 2023 | Pakistan 2000 → 2023 |
|---|---|---|
| GDP Growth (annual avg) | 5.1 % | 3.7 % |
| Exports (USD bn) | 62 → 289 | 9 → 31 |

| | | |
|---|---|---|
| Current Account (% GDP) | +1.3 avg | −4.5 avg |
| Investment Rate (% GDP) | 32 → 33 | 17 → 14 |
| Poverty Rate (US $3.65 PPP) | 61 % → 6.5 % | 43 % → 35 % |
| Corruption Perception Index (score 100) | 19 → 38 | 23 → 28 |

## 9 Policy Lessons for Pakistan (2025–2035)

1. Anchor stability in rules, not loans. Adopt Fiscal Responsibility Act (3 % deficit cap).
2. Create Export Diversification Fund for non-textile value chains (agro-processing, engineering).
3. Reform SOEs: shift from political appointments to performance contracts.
4. TVET modernization via public-private boards.
5. Regional industrial clusters around logistics corridors (Karachi-Lahore, Gwadar-Quetta).
6. Digital tax administration to raise tax-GDP to 15 %.
7. Green downstreaming: use domestic minerals (lithium, copper) for EV components.

## 10 Conclusion — The Economy as Institution

The difference between Indonesia and Pakistan is not resource endowment but institutional coherence. Indonesia learned to bind elites through law; Pakistan continues to free elites through exception. Macroeconomic resilience emerges when rules survive elections.

For Pakistan, escaping the "stabilization trap" requires transforming the Ministry of Finance from a cashier into a coordination hub—linking budgets, industrial policy, and human-capital strategy. Economic sovereignty lies not in isolation but in predictability.

# References

Asian Development Bank. (2024). *Industrial Transformation in Southeast Asia.* Manila.

Bank Indonesia. (2023). *Annual Report.* Jakarta.

Hausmann, R., & Hidalgo, C. (2020). *Atlas of Economic Complexity.* Harvard CID.

IMF. (2024). *World Economic Outlook Database.*

Khan, M. (2010). *Rents, Rent-Seeking and Economic Development.* Cambridge University Press.

Nasution, A. (2016). *Indonesia's Macroeconomic Reform Agenda.* ADBI Working Paper No. 601.

Pakistan Bureau of Statistics. (2024). *Economic Survey of Pakistan.* Islamabad.

UNIDO. (2024). *Industrial Development Report 2024.*

World Bank. (2024). *World Development Indicators.*

# Chapter 4

## Social Foundations — How Indonesia Built Legitimacy through Human Development, and What Pakistan Can Replicate

## 1 Abstract

This chapter argues that the legitimacy of democratic governance in a majority-Muslim society depends less on ideology than on the state's ability to guarantee basic human dignity—education, health, and social protection. Indonesia's post-1998 "social contract of inclusion" transformed citizen expectations and re-anchored democracy after decades of authoritarian rule.

Using comparable data from the World Bank (WDI), UNDP (HDR Index 2024), WHO, and national surveys, the chapter traces how Indonesia expanded literacy from 86 to 97 percent, reduced infant mortality from 46 to 18 per 1 000, and achieved gender-parity in school enrollment. By contrast, Pakistan—despite constitutional guarantees—continues to under-invest in human development, spending barely 2 percent of GDP on education and 0.9 percent on health.

The central claim: social development is not an adjunct to democracy; it is its infrastructure.
Without visible public dividends in health, schooling, and safety, no constitutional clause can sustain legitimacy.

## 2 Introduction — Human Development as Political Legitimacy

In the Asian context, the concept of a "developmental state" has often implied coercion. Indonesia after 1998 redefined it as a participatory developmental state—one that earns its right to govern through service delivery.

During the Suharto era (1967–1998), state legitimacy rested on growth averaging 7 percent per year but concentrated in Java's urban core. When

36

the 1997 Asian financial crisis eroded that compact, the Reformasi leaders realized that democracy would not survive without a tangible redistribution of public goods. Hence, between 1999 and 2014, social spending rose from 7 to 19 percent of the budget.

In Pakistan, by contrast, state legitimacy remains attached to security narratives and religious symbolism rather than to service delivery. The result is a chronic cycle of low trust and high expectation. According to the Gallup Pakistan Social Trust Survey (2023), only 27 percent of citizens believe that the state cares about their well-being, the lowest rate in South Asia.

The chapter thus frames human development as a political instrument as much as a moral imperative.

## 3 Indonesia's Post-1998 Social-Policy Revolution

Reformasi's first Cabinet (1999) adopted a simple rule: "Decentralize resources, centralize standards."
Three laws anchored this principle:

1. Law No. 22/1999 on Regional Governance – transferred basic education and health to district governments.
2. Law No. 25/1999 on Fiscal Balance – established block grants (Dana Alokasi Umum) to fund local services.
3. Law No. 32/2004 – introduced direct local elections, creating democratic accountability for service provision.

Between 2001 and 2010, Indonesia built more than 40 000 new schools and 15 000 community health centers (*puskesmas*). Social protection programs followed: the *Jamkesmas* (2005) health card, the *BOS* school operational grant (2005), and conditional cash transfers through *PKH* (2007).

By 2019, these schemes covered over 65 million people—nearly one-quarter of the population—and were absorbed into the universal insurance system *BPJS Kesehatan*. Spending on health rose to 1.7 percent of GDP (WHO 2024), education to 3.8 percent, and social assistance to 1.2 percent.

The impact was not only quantitative. By empowering district heads (*bupati*), Reformasi created a new political class whose electoral success depended on school buildings, clinics, and roads rather than patronage alone.

## 4 Education — The Long Game of Nation-Building

### 4.1 Access and Equity

In 2003, the Indonesian Constitution was amended to mandate education spending of at least 20 percent of the national budget. This legal anchor shielded education funding from political volatility. As a result:

- Net enrollment in primary school rose to 99 percent by 2018.
- Lower-secondary enrollment climbed from 62 to 91 percent.
- Gender parity index reached 1.01 (World Bank 2024).

Crucially, Indonesia's education policy emphasized equalization across districts, not elite expansion. The *BOS* grant flows directly to school accounts based on student numbers, reducing scope for leakage.

Pakistan, meanwhile, spends less than 2 percent of GDP on education, half of it on teacher salaries with minimal learning outcomes. ASER 2023 found that only 38 percent of grade five students could read a story in Urdu or English, compared to 91 percent literacy among Indonesian fourth-graders (UNESCO 2023).

### 4.2 Curriculum and Civic Identity

Indonesia rewrote its curriculum (2006 and 2013) around "Character Education (*Pendidikan Karakter*)" and the five principles of *Pancasila*. Rather than religious indoctrination, the focus shifted to pluralism, honesty, and civic ethics.

By contrast, Pakistan's Single National Curriculum (SNC) 2021 has been criticized for re-centralizing ideological control and undermining provincial innovation (UNDP Policy Note 2023). Educational pluralism remains fragmented between madrassas, private English-medium, and public Urdu-medium systems.

## 4.3 Teacher Quality and Decentralized Oversight

Indonesia's teacher certification program (2005) required a four-year degree and competency exam for salary increments. This professionalization increased motivation and reduced absenteeism from 19 to 8 percent (World Bank 2022).

Pakistan's teacher absenteeism averages 24 percent (ILO 2023), partly because monitoring is hierarchical rather than community-based. Replicating Indonesia's *School Committee Model* (*Komite Sekolah*) could improve accountability and public ownership.

## 5 Health — Universal Coverage and Local Accountability

Indonesia recognized early that health is both a public service and a symbol of citizenship. The creation of *BPJS Kesehatan* (2014) merged all previous insurance schemes into one national pool, funded by payroll taxes and state subsidies for the poor.

Key results (WHO 2024):

- Life expectancy increased from 67 to 72 years (2000–2023).
- Infant mortality fell from 46 to 18 per 1 000 live births.
- Maternal mortality ratio declined from 265 to 126 per 100 000.

Decentralized accountability was critical: districts manage hospitals but must report standardized health indicators to the Ministry of Health. Performance grants reward improvement.

Pakistan spends only 0.9 percent of GDP on health (WHO 2023) and relies heavily on donor-funded vertical programs. Infant mortality remains at 55 per 1 000; maternal mortality at 186. The Sehat Sahulat card scheme (2016) is an important step but covers barely 10 percent of the population and lacks hospital capacity in rural areas.

Indonesia's lesson is institutional, not financial: a nationwide insurance system works only when data, funding, and accountability are linked at the district level.

## 6 Gender and Inclusion — From Symbolic to Structural

Indonesia's reforms after 1998 framed gender equality not as "women's affairs" but as a governance indicator.
The 2000 Presidential Instruction No. 9 on *Gender Mainstreaming* required every ministry to include measurable gender outcomes in its budget.
By 2020:

- Women held 21 percent of parliamentary seats (vs. only 9 percent in 1999).
- Female labor-force participation reached 54 percent (WB 2024).
- 80 percent of public hospitals were headed by women in senior administrative roles.

Civil-society partnerships—particularly *Aisyiyah* (Muhammadiyah women's wing) and *Fatayat NU*—linked Islamic ethics to social-justice goals, softening religious resistance.
This made gender equality appear indigenous, not imposed.

Pakistan's gender reforms have remained largely symbolic:
reserved legislative seats have not translated into policy authority, and patriarchal norms continue to constrain women's economic mobility.
Female labor-force participation stagnates near 22 percent;
only 10 percent of civil-service officers are women (FBS 2024).
The *Benazir Income Support Programme (BISP)* is a vital safety net but not a ladder of empowerment; its cash grants cover consumption rather than skill-building.

The lesson from Indonesia is that gender equality must be embedded in budgeting, service delivery, and local decision-making, not confined to representation quotas.


## 7 Pakistan's Human-Capital Paradox

Despite a young population—median age 20.6 years—Pakistan faces an education–employment disjunction.
Each year nearly 4 million youths enter the labor force, yet fewer than 500 000 formal jobs are created (ILO 2024).
Skills mismatch, poor health, and gender exclusion collectively depress productivity.

Key constraints include:

- Fragmented governance: Education and health devolved to provinces (18th Amendment 2010) without fiscal alignment.
- Elite capture: 40 percent of federal scholarships go to students from the top income quintile (UNDP 2023).
- Low credibility of public services: 41 percent of parents pay for private tutoring even in government-school catchments (ASER 2023).

This paradox—youth abundance without human capital—translates into macroeconomic fragility:
under-skilled labor limits export diversification, constraining foreign-exchange earnings and increasing debt dependence.

The "human-capital dividend" can thus easily become a liability if not harnessed through coordinated education–industry policy.

# 8 Quantitative Comparison (2000 – 2024)

| Indicator | Indonesia | Pakistan |
|---|---|---|
| Literacy Rate (%) | 86 → 97 | 53 → 62 |
| Infant Mortality (per 1 000) | 46 → 18 | 86 → 55 |
| Maternal Mortality (per 100 000) | 265 → 126 | 276 → 186 |
| Life Expectancy (yrs) | 67 → 72 | 63 → 67 |
| Public Health Expenditure (% GDP) | 0.9 → 1.7 | 0.7 → 0.9 |
| Education Expenditure (% GDP) | 2.2 → 3.8 | 1.8 → 2.0 |
| Gender Parity in Schooling (Index) | 0.89 → 1.01 | 0.74 → 0.86 |
| Poverty Headcount (% ≤ $3.65 PPP) | 61 → 6.5 | 43 → 35 |
| Citizen Trust in Govt (%) | 59 | 27 |

The data reveal a simple pattern:
where social investment rises, political legitimacy deepens.
Indonesia's social-spending surge after 2001 produced a virtuous cycle—
trust → tax compliance → resources → better services—
whereas Pakistan remains stuck in the opposite loop of mistrust and underfunding.

# 9 Policy Roadmap (2025 – 2035)

## 1 . Constitutionalize social rights.

Amend Article 9 to define the right to health and education as *justiciable*, not aspirational.

## 2 . Fiscal guarantees.

Legislate a *Social Sector Floor*: minimum 4 percent of GDP for education, 2 percent for health.

## 3 . National Human Capital Authority (NHCA).

Coordinate data, forecasting, and workforce planning across ministries; publish a bi-annual *Human Capital Dashboard*.

**4 . District performance grants.**

Allocate transfers based on literacy, immunization, and gender-parity improvements—replicating Indonesia's *DAK Performance Incentives*.

**5 . Universal Primary Healthcare Network.**

Merge vertical programs into a *National Primary Care Agency* with integrated electronic records.

**6 . Skills for industry alignment.**

Link TVET curricula to export sectors (textiles, engineering, IT); introduce dual training with private partners.

**7 . Women's Economic Agency Fund.**

Shift BISP from consumption support to entrepreneurship grants, training, and market linkages.

**8 . Civic education revamp.**

Embed human-rights and constitutional literacy in school curricula to build citizen identity beyond sectarian lines.

**9 . Digital public services.**

Scale up the *NADRA–Ehsaas* platform for health, education, and cash transfers using one citizen ID.

## 10 . Monitoring and public reporting.

Mandate annual "Social Accountability Reports" by Parliament and provincial assemblies with media access.

These reforms require not just money but political imagination — a shift from security to human security as the core national mission.


## 10 Conclusion — Social Trust as the True Currency of the State

Indonesia's democratic endurance stems from an invisible capital: trust.
Each school built, each midwife trained, each conditional-cash-transfer delivered became a micro-contract between state and citizen.
Legitimacy accumulated not by rhetoric but by reliability.

Pakistan's path to resilience lies not in larger armies or aid packages but in credible public services.
When citizens see fairness in education, dignity in healthcare, and equality in opportunity,
they defend the constitution instinctively because it defends them.

As one Indonesian reformer said in 2004,

"We rebuilt faith in democracy not with words, but with clinics."

For Pakistan and its peers, that remains the ultimate blueprint: governance as care.

## References (APA Format)

ASER Pakistan. (2023). *Annual Status of Education Report.* Lahore.

Asian Development Bank. (2024). *Human Capital and Resilience in Asia.* Manila.

Gallup Pakistan. (2023). *Social Trust Survey 2023.*

ILO. (2024). *Employment Outlook for South Asia 2024.* Geneva.

UNDP. (2023). *Human Development Report — Pakistan Country Brief.*

UNESCO. (2023). *Global Education Monitoring Report.*

UN Women. (2024). *Gender Mainstreaming in Indonesia.* Jakarta.

WHO. (2024). *World Health Statistics 2024.* Geneva.

World Bank. (2022). *Indonesia Teacher Certification Impact Study.*

World Bank. (2024). *World Development Indicators 2024.*

# Chapter 5

## Money, Debt, and Shocks — Indonesia's Crisis-Management Playbook vs. Pakistan's Stop-Go Stabilization

## 1 Abstract

This chapter contrasts two monetary and fiscal trajectories after repeated external shocks.

Indonesia transformed the trauma of 1997–98 into a rules-based fiscal regime and built buffers that made later crises survivable.

Pakistan, despite decades of IMF programs, still alternates between boom and bust because fiscal institutions remain politicized and debt unsupervised.

> Crisis management is not about firefighting; it is about building a fire-resistant house.

The chapter demonstrates that credible rules, automatic stabilizers, and transparent debt ceilings can convert volatility into resilience.

## 2 Historical Context: From Panic to Policy

### 2.1 Indonesia 1997–2008: Building Credibility

- GDP collapsed –13 % (1998); currency depreciated > 80 %.
- Within five years, inflation fell from 77 % to 6 %, reserves rebuilt from $18 billion → $110 billion.
- The State Finance Law (17/2003), State Treasury Law (1/2004), and Fiscal Balance Law (33/2004) together imposed a *3 % deficit ceiling* and *60 % debt-to-GDP cap*.
- The Fiscal Policy Agency (BKF) became an analytic center to test every subsidy or bailout against these limits.

By 2008, public debt/GDP had dropped to 32 %. When the global crisis hit, Indonesia could deploy counter-cyclical spending without losing investor confidence.

## 2.2 Pakistan 2008–2023: The Loop of Stabilization

• Since 1958, Pakistan has entered 23 IMF arrangements; the average interval between programs is 3 years.

• Each program promised "fiscal discipline," yet tax revenue remained around 9–11 % of GDP.

• Political turnovers repeatedly suspended reforms—particularly in energy pricing and SOE restructuring.

• The 2019 EBA brought short-term stability but no structural credibility; by 2023, debt-service consumed 57 % of federal revenue.

## 3 Anatomy of the Stop-Go Cycle

| Stage | Policy Reaction | Outcome |
|---|---|---|
| Boom | Subsidized fuel, overvalued rupee | Import surge, reserves fall |
| Warning | IMF standby, monetary tightening | Growth slump |
| Adjustment fatigue | Election cycle spending | Inflation rebound |
| Crisis | External rollover blocked | Devaluation, aid request |
| Repeat | – | – |

The absence of binding fiscal rules turns every cabinet into a new experiment.
Debt sustainability is judged politically, not mathematically.

## 4 Fiscal Institutions: Why Rules Worked in Indonesia

1. Legal ceilings. The 3 %/60 % rules are statutory, not executive guidelines.

2. Transparency law (15/2004). Annual audit by the *Badan Pemeriksa Keuangan (BPK)* submitted to Parliament.

3. Inter-ministerial coordination. Finance, Planning, and Bank Indonesia operate a *Macroeconomic Framework (MKF)*—updated quarterly with public forecasts.

4. Medium-Term Expenditure Framework (MTEF). Rolling three-year ceilings make budgets predictable.

5. Sub-national discipline. Local governments barred from foreign borrowing without Finance Ministry consent.

Indonesia thereby created a feedback loop where credibility lowered borrowing costs, freeing space for social spending.

## 5 Monetary Policy and Central-Bank Independence

- Bank Indonesia Act (23/1999, amended 2004): established price stability as the single mandate.
- Governors hold five-year staggered terms; dismissal requires parliamentary approval.
- Inflation targeting (since 2005) reduced average CPI volatility from ±10 p.p. to ±3 p.p.

Pakistan's State Bank Act (1956, amended 2021) nominally grants autonomy but political directives persist.
Ad hoc exchange-rate interventions eroded reserves—2022 depletion from $20 billion → $3 billion.

Autonomy without accountability breeds arrogance; autonomy with transparency breeds stability.

## 6 Debt Composition and Management

Indonesia

- External debt ≈ 30 % of GDP, mostly long-term concessional.

- Domestic bond market (government securities > $200 billion) attracts pension funds and insurers.
- Debt-management office (DJPPR) publishes monthly risk reports and maturity profiles.

Pakistan

- Public debt ≈ 77 % of GDP (2024); one-third in short-term T-Bills.
- Domestic banks hold > 70 % of government securities—crowding out private credit.
- No unified debt-management agency; reporting fragmented across SBP and Finance Ministry.

Result:  average interest cost 10–12 %, vs Indonesia's 5 %.

## 7  Shock Absorbers: Reserves, Safety Nets, and Credibility

**Indonesia used crises to create *automatic stabilizers*:**

| Instrument | Mechanism | Coverage |
|---|---|---|
| Budget Stabilization Fund (2009) | windfall resource revenue saved | trigger = > 2 % GDP swing |
| Fuel-subsidy compensation (2005–2014) | cash transfers to poor during price hikes | 19 million HHs |
| Unemployment & health insurance (BPJS) | linked contributions | 80 % formal labor |
| Contingent credit line (WB/ADB) | disburses if natural disaster or capital flight | $5 bn buffer |

Pakistan's buffers remain discretionary: ad-hoc relief packages, donor-funded schemes, and politically timed subsidies.
Hence each shock—whether COVID-19 or 2022 floods—translates directly into fiscal stress.

## 8 Energy and Exchange-Rate Governance

Indonesia phased out generalized fuel subsidies (2005–2014) and redirected savings to education and infrastructure ($\approx$ 3 % GDP).
Pakistan's energy pricing remains the core fiscal drain:
circular debt > PKR 2.6 trillion ($\approx$ 3 % GDP, 2024).
Tariffs below cost keep losses rolling into new loans.

Exchange-rate management follows the same pattern: Indonesia adopted a free-float with limited intervention; Pakistan's managed float often serves political timing.
Currency overvaluation, once 15–20 %, cripples exports and favors import lobbies.

## 9 Empirical Snapshot (2023)

| Indicator | Indonesia | Pakistan |
|---|---|---|
| Fiscal deficit (% GDP) | 2.3 | 7.7 |
| Public debt (% GDP) | 38 | 77 |
| Inflation (%) | 3.1 | 28 |
| FX reserves (months import) | 6.2 | 0.9 |
| Tax revenue (% GDP) | 12.2 | 9.3 |
| Current account (% GDP) | −0.5 | −4.4 |
| Social spending (% budget) | 19 | 9 |

**Numbers tell a single story: rules + credibility = resilience.**

## 10 Policy Lessons and Roadmap (2025–2035)

### 1 Fiscal Responsibility Law

– Embed 3 % deficit / 60 % debt caps in statute, not MoU.
– Create a non-partisan *Fiscal Council* to publish mid-year reviews.

## 2 Unified Debt-Management Office

– Merge SBP and Finance debt cells; publish quarterly risk matrix.
– Shift to 70 % domestic-long tenor composition by 2030.

## 3 Medium-Term Budgeting

– Adopt rolling three-year ceilings; enforce expenditure classification by outcome.

## 4 Stabilization Fund

– Channel 20 % of any resource or remittance windfall into a sovereign buffer.

## 5 Transparency & Audit

– Annual "Citizen Budget" and independent *Public Accounts Committee* hearings broadcast live.

## 6 Energy-Pricing Reform

– Replace blanket subsidies with targeted digital transfers (linked to NADRA-Ehsaas).

## 7 Exchange-Rate Credibility Pact

– Pre-announce SBP intervention bands; publish daily FX data.

## 8 Financial Inclusion

– Expand mobile-banking base to 100 million accounts by 2030; tie savings incentives to government securities.

## 9 Social Shock Absorbers

– Scale up *BISP* → *Social Insurance Authority* covering illness & unemployment.

## 10 Data Integrity Charter

– Ensure public access to fiscal & debt dashboards (machine-readable).

## 11 Conclusion: From Program Dependence to Policy Sovereignty

Indonesia's transformation shows that sovereignty is not a speech—it is a spreadsheet.
When rules are credible and transparent, markets reward discipline with lower costs, and citizens reward it with trust.

Pakistan can escape its *stop-go treadmill* only by depoliticizing the budget and professionalizing the institutions that guard it.
Stability must become an internal habit, not an external condition.

> To borrow less, Pakistan must first borrow credibility from its own citizens.

# References

Asian Development Bank. (2024). *Fiscal Rules and Resilience in Emerging Asia.* Manila.

Bank Indonesia. (2023). *Annual Report 2023.* Jakarta.

IMF. (2024). *World Economic Outlook Database.*

Ministry of Finance (Indonesia). (2024). *Fiscal Risk Statement.*

Pakistan Bureau of Statistics. (2024). *Economic Survey of Pakistan 2023-24.* Islamabad.

State Bank of Pakistan. (2024). *Annual Report.* Karachi.

UNDP. (2023). *Macroeconomic Governance and Human Security.* New York.

World Bank. (2024). *World Development Indicators.*

World Bank. (2022). *Indonesia Public Expenditure Review.*

# Chapter 6

## The Uniform and the Republic — Civil–Military Balance as the Core of Constitutional Order

### 1 Abstract

For half a century, Pakistan's uniform has symbolized both discipline and dominance.
Indonesia's once did the same—until the 1998 Reformasi stripped the military of its "dual function" and re-anchored national defense in law, not loyalty.

This chapter argues that civil–military balance is not a matter of etiquette but of constitutional architecture.
When soldiers know the limits of lawful command, and civilians learn the duties of lawful oversight, the republic becomes self-correcting.

### 2 Historical Backdrop: Two Republics, Two Paths

#### Indonesia

Under Suharto's *Dwifungsi ABRI* doctrine (1966-1998), the armed forces wielded a "dual function": security + socio-political guidance.
ABRI officers occupied 75 parliamentary seats, ran ministries, and controlled provincial governments.

#### After the 1997–98 crisis, reformers dismantled this system:

- 1999 – Abolition of reserved military seats in the People's Consultative Assembly (MPR).
- 2000 – Separation of the Police from the Armed Forces (Law 2/2002).
- 2004 – TNI Law 34/2004 restricted the military to external defense only.

- 2005–09 – Closure of all military-owned businesses and foundations.

Result: a professional force, smaller budget share (≈ 0.8 % GDP), and sharply reduced political intervention.

## Pakistan

The military has ruled directly for 31 of the country's first 76 years, and indirectly for the rest.
The *National Security Council, ISPR*, and military-owned conglomerates (*Fauji Foundation, Bahria Town, Askari Group*) constitute what Pakistani scholars call *Milbus*—"military business."
Even after the 2008 return to civilian rule, the army's budget and internal deployment remain opaque.

## 3 Measuring the Balance

| Indicator | Indonesia (2023) | Pakistan (2023) |
|---|---|---|
| Defense spending (% GDP) | 0.8 | 2.7 |
| Paramilitary share of security forces | 22 % | 54 % |
| Internal deployments (avg days/year) | < 30 | > 250 |
| Civilian oversight committee budget power | Strong (Parliamentary Commission I) | Weak (National Assembly Defence Committee advisory only) |
| Prosecution of unlawful orders (2015-23) | 9 cases | 0 |

**Numbers reveal an imbalance of accountability rather than of firepower.**

## 4  Legal Frameworks and Their Logic

### Indonesia's Model

### The 1945 Constitution as amended (Art. 30) states:

> *"The Indonesian National Armed Forces shall defend the state against external threats and shall not engage in political affairs."*

TNI Law 34/2004 clarifies:

- Internal deployment only under Presidential decree + Parliamentary notification.
- Military courts subordinate to civil courts for crimes against civilians.
- Inspector-General system for discipline and whistle-blower protection.

### Pakistan's Gap

Article 245 of Pakistan's Constitution allows the armed forces to "act in aid of civil power," but without statutory criteria or judicial review.
This single phrase has justified decades of internal policing—from FATA to Karachi.
Civilian governments invoke it for convenience; the military invokes it for autonomy.

## 5  The Doctrine of Lawful Refusal

### Modern militaries operate on two complementary duties:

1. Duty to Obey lawful orders.
2. Duty to Disobey manifestly unlawful orders.

Germany, Israel, and Indonesia embed this in training manuals.
It derives from Nuremberg Principle IV: "Orders from a superior do not exempt a person from responsibility if the order was manifestly illegal."

A professional soldier is not a political tool but a moral agent.
Refusal of illegal orders protects both citizens and the integrity of the army.

## 6 Case Studies

### Indonesia 2001 — Ambon and Poso

When sectarian violence flared, the TNI command refused provincial governors' ad-hoc calls for "total military operations," insisting on parliamentary authorization.
That precedent institutionalized the principle of civilian trigger control.

### Pakistan 2014 — Operation Zarb-e-Azb

Launched by executive order under Article 245, without parliamentary debate or post-operation audit.
Collateral damage data remain classified; no civilian oversight mechanism was activated.
The army gained tactical success but strategic impunity.

## 7 Economic Footprint of Milbus

| Domain | Indonesia (1998) | Indonesia (2023) | Pakistan (2023) |
|---|---|---|---|
| Military-owned enterprises | 220 | 0 (formally liquidated) | > 50 |
| Off-budget holdings (% defense assets) | > 20 % | < 1 % | ≈ 25 % |
| Public audit coverage | Comprehensive | Annual BPK audit | Partial MoD internal audit only |

**The economic power of the uniform is political power in disguise.**
**Transparency is not a threat to security—it is the price of legitimacy.**

## 8 Rebalancing Mechanisms for Pakistan

1.  **Constitutional Amendment:**
Codify that internal deployment requires parliamentary approval + judicial review within 30 days.

2.  **Defence Budget Transparency:**
Shift from lump-sum to program-based appropriations audited by the Auditor General.

3.  **Parliamentary Defence Committee Reform:**
Grant summons and budget scrutiny powers (equal to PAC).

4.  **Inspector-General for the Armed Forces:**
Independent office for complaints and whistle-blower protection.

5.  **Professional Education:**
Integrate international humanitarian law and constitutional ethics into military curricula.

6.  **Gradual Demilitarization of Civil Agencies:**
Police, NADRA, and disaster response to return to civilian leadership within five years.

## 9 Normative Shift: From Obedience to Conscience

Discipline is a virtue only when guided by law.
Blind obedience creates efficient tyrannies;
law-conscious obedience creates republican armies.

"The honor of a soldier lies not in silence, but in lawful service." — Indonesian Military Academy Motto (2006)

For Pakistan, moral courage must replace political loyalty as the supreme military value.

# 10 Comparative Snapshot

| Dimension | Indonesia | Pakistan |
|---|---|---|
| Legal mandate for internal deployment | Statutory, reviewable | Constitutional ambiguity |
| Civilian oversight institutions | Strong (BPK, Komisi I) | Weak & ad-hoc |
| Military business holdings | Dissolved | Expanding |
| Press freedom on defence issues | High | Restricted |
| Training on lawful refusal | Mandatory | Absent |

**The gap is not cultural—it is institutional.**

# 11 Policy Blueprint (2026–2035)

1. Adopt a "Civilian Supremacy and Lawful Refusal Article" (see draft in Preface).

2. Mandate annual defence white paper with spending and deployment details.

3. Civil-military liaison council to coordinate disaster response under civil chairmanship.

4. Audit of military-linked SOEs and foundations, followed by gradual divestiture.

5. Integration of retired officers into civil roles through merit-based public service exams, not quotas.

6. Public reporting dashboard for defence expenditure and disciplinary cases.

7. Regional confidence-building with Indonesia & Malaysia on defence ethics and training exchange.

## 12 Conclusion: When the Gun Returns to the Barracks

Indonesia proved that a military need not be humiliated to be civilized—it must be professionalized.
Pakistan can do the same if the uniform accepts that its greatest honor is to defend the law, not replace it.

> A republic is secure when its soldiers obey the constitution more faithfully than its rulers do.

## References (APA)

Crouch, H. (2010). *Political Reform in Indonesia after Suharto.* ISEAS.

International Crisis Group. (2023). *Pakistan's Civil–Military Relations.* Brussels.

Kingsbury, D. (2018). *Power Politics and the Indonesian Military.* Routledge.

Siddiqa, A. (2007). *Military Inc.: Inside Pakistan's Military Economy.* Oxford University Press.

UNDP. (2024). *Security Sector Governance in Asia.* New York.

World Bank. (2023). *Governance Indicators Dataset.*

# Chapter 7

## Cities, Dignity, and the Daily State — From Fear-Based Policing to Rights-Based Governance

## 1 Abstract

A republic is not tested in its capitals but in its cities — in how the daily state touches ordinary lives.
Where people meet the government most directly — the police station, the municipal office, the bus stop — the legitimacy of the entire system is decided.

This chapter examines how Indonesia's post-1998 decentralization transformed local governance, policing, and service delivery, turning fear into civic dignity.
In contrast, Pakistan's cities — from Karachi to Lahore, Quetta to Peshawar — still operate under a fragmented and coercive "colonial inheritance" model.

The argument is simple:

> To rebuild national trust, the state must become visible not as power, but as service.

## 2 The Daily Face of the State

For most citizens, "government" is not parliament or cabinet; it is the officer who stops a bus, the clerk who stamps a paper, the policeman who demands or defers a bribe.
Daily contact — not grand reform — shapes legitimacy.

In Indonesia, the 2001 "Big Bang Decentralization" transferred more than 25,000 functions to local governments.
Municipalities gained authority over:

- Primary education and health
- Local roads, markets, and transport
- Community policing and dispute resolution

In Pakistan, by contrast, the 18th Amendment (2010) devolved power from center to provinces — but not from provinces to districts. Citizens remain distant from decision-making; every complaint must climb bureaucratic stairs.

## 3 Policing: From Control to Protection

### Indonesia's Shift

In 2000, the police (Polri) were separated from the military and placed under civilian control.
Their motto changed from *"Mengamankan negara"* ("Securing the state")
to *"Melindungi dan melayani masyarakat"* ("Protecting and serving the people").

### Reforms included:

- Community policing (Polmas) units in every subdistrict
- Complaint desks and mobile service vans
- Training in mediation, domestic violence, and traffic ethics

By 2022, 67% of Indonesians reported "high trust" in local police (LSI survey), compared to 21% in 1998.

### Pakistan's Stagnation

Pakistan Police Order (2002) created public safety commissions and complaint authorities,
but they remain toothless.
Frequent postings, political interference, and lack of funds reduce police morale.

The police are seen less as protectors than as enforcers of the powerful.
A 2023 Gallup survey found only 24% of citizens expressed trust in police —
the lowest among South Asian peers.

## 4 Local Justice and ADR (Alternative Dispute Resolution)

In Indonesia, local councils (desa adat, musyawarah) mediate over 60% of
rural disputes.
They combine tradition and due process, often preventing escalation into
violence.
State courts recognize these settlements if documented and consensual.

Pakistan's *jirga* and *panchayat* traditions play similar roles but remain
outside the formal legal system, often dominated by elites and gender bias.
Legal integration — not abolition — is key.
By granting statutory recognition under the judiciary's supervision, Pakistan
could turn informal justice into legitimate "first contact justice."

## 5 Municipal Services and Urban Dignity

### Indonesia

### Decentralization allowed cities to innovate:

- *Surabaya* introduced participatory budgeting: citizens vote on local projects.
- *Bandung* digitized permit systems and created "24-hour complaint apps."
- *Makassar* launched *"Smart City"* dashboards for waste, traffic, and crime mapping.

Citizens saw visible change — fewer lines, more lights, cleaner streets.
Municipal dignity became national legitimacy.

## Pakistan

City governance remains politically hostage:

- Karachi's mayoral system frequently suspended by provincial authorities.
- Lahore's "Metropolitan Corporation" exists on paper but lacks fiscal autonomy.
- Urban service budgets are diverted to prestige projects (flyovers, monuments).

The result: solid waste crises, unlit streets, flooding, and chronic distrust.


## 6 Dignity as Policy Variable

Development economists measure GDP; citizens measure dignity per day.

**Dignity has three dimensions:**

| Dimension | Description | Indonesia | Pakistan |
|---|---|---|---|
| Procedural | Can I get a service without humiliation? | Moderate → High | Low |
| Spatial | Does my neighborhood reflect equality? | Visible progress | Declining |
| Psychological | Do I feel safe and respected by officials? | Improved | Worsened |

In Indonesia, every local office was mandated to publish a "citizen charter": expected waiting time, fee structure, officer name.
In Pakistan, citizens still face discretionary gatekeeping.

When humiliation is normalized, law loses moral authority.

# 7 Data Snapshot — Trust and the Local State

| Indicator | Indonesia 1998 → 2023 | Pakistan 1998 → 2023 |
| --- | --- | --- |
| Trust in police (%) | 21 → 67 | 38 → 24 |
| Trust in local government (%) | 29 → 72 | 41 → 33 |
| Urban service satisfaction (%) | 22 → 68 | 30 → 35 |
| Perceived corruption in local offices (lower is better) | 78 → 42 | 66 → 70 |

(LSI Indonesia, Gallup Pakistan, Transparency Int'l 2023)

# 8 The Institutional Logic

**Indonesia:**

- Decentralization backed by fiscal autonomy (DAU/DAK transfers).
- Performance-based grants: cities scored on service delivery.
- Mayors directly elected; citizens could punish inefficiency.

**Pakistan:**

- Provinces reluctant to share revenue or power.
- Local elections irregular, often postponed.
- Bureaucrats answer upward, not outward.

The difference is "vertical loyalty" vs. "horizontal accountability."

# 9 Policy Recommendations (2025–2035)

1. Revive and strengthen district governments under a new *Local Governance Act* ensuring fiscal and administrative independence.

66

2. Create municipal police under mayors, trained in mediation and community engagement.

3. Launch a "Citizen Dignity Charter" — standardized service timelines and complaint redressal across departments.

4. Digitize all city services (permits, taxes, birth certificates) under a single mobile portal.

5. Integrate ADR centers under district judiciary with state funding.

6. Reform police evaluation — performance based on citizen trust, not FIR count.

7. Establish urban equity index measuring service gaps between neighborhoods.

8. Institute annual "City Report Cards" published by National Statistics Bureau.

9. Link provincial grants to citizen satisfaction surveys.

10. Public service training in ethics and empathy.


## 10 Conclusion — When the State Learns to Serve

No nation becomes democratic merely by holding elections;
it becomes democratic when people feel respected in daily transactions.
Indonesia's lesson is not only decentralization but humanization of governance.
When a poor street vendor in Bandung can speak to an officer without fear, the republic breathes.

**Pakistan's urban future depends on one transformation:**

From fear-based control to dignity-based citizenship.

The republic that learns to say *"I serve"* instead of *"I order"*
will outlive any regime.

## References (APA)

Asia Foundation. (2023). *Indonesia–Pakistan Local Governance Survey.*

Buehler, M. (2010). *Decentralisation and Local Democracy in Indonesia.* Routledge.

Cheema, A., Khwaja, A., & Qadir, A. (2019). *Local Government Reforms in Pakistan: A Comparative Analysis.* Harvard Kennedy School.

LSI Indonesia. (2023). *Public Trust Barometer.*

Transparency International. (2023). *Global Corruption Barometer.*

UNDP. (2024). *Urban Governance and Human Dignity Index.*

World Bank. (2024). *World Development Indicators.*

# Chapter 8

## Provinces → Districts: Where Legitimacy Lives

### 1. Abstract

The state's legitimacy does not reside in its constitution alone — it is performed at the district level.
That is where citizens most tangibly experience justice, services, and fairness;
where the flag becomes either a symbol of trust or a reminder of distance.

Indonesia's "big-bang" decentralization after 1999 empowered over 440 districts (kabupaten/kota) with both administrative and fiscal autonomy, reshaping the daily social contract.
Pakistan's 18th Amendment (2010) devolved powers to provinces but stopped halfway — the district, where people actually live, remained institutionally starved.

This chapter argues that Pakistan's next reform frontier must be district-level compacts: local governments with real budgets, measurable outcomes, and citizen scorecards, aligned to transparent federal and provincial transfers.
That is where the republic's credibility will either heal or collapse.

### 2. The District as the Republic's Frontline

Every modern state, regardless of its constitutional form, has a single point of truth:

> *"Do citizens feel the state exists for them?"*

> In Pakistan, the distance between voter and service is vast.
> The average citizen interacts more with a patwari or police constable than with any elected representative.

69

Provincial capitals — Lahore, Karachi, Quetta, Peshawar — absorb power but not accountability.

Indonesia learned the same lesson earlier.
Before 1998, Jakarta dictated everything: teacher postings, health budgets, irrigation repairs.
When the system collapsed during the Asian crisis, decentralization became a survival mechanism.

By 2004, every Indonesian district had:

- An elected regent (bupati) or mayor (walikota);
- Its own budget, planning board, and audit office;
- Authority over education, health, agriculture, infrastructure, and licensing.

From that moment, legitimacy began to live close to home.


## 3. Fiscal Architecture: Following the Money

### Indonesia's Model

The 2001 decentralization laws (Law 22/1999, Law 25/1999, later updated 32/2004 and 33/2004) established three main transfers:

| Instrument | Purpose | Formula Principle |
|---|---|---|
| DAU – General Allocation Fund | Equalization across regions | Population, area, fiscal gap |
| DAK – Special Allocation Fund | National priority programs | Sector-based needs (health, education, infrastructure) |
| Revenue Sharing (DBH) | Local share of taxes & natural resources | % of origin-based revenue |

Districts receive about 35% of the national budget via these formulas.
Transfers are predictable, rules-based, and public.

## Pakistan's Structure

Pakistan's National Finance Commission (NFC) Award governs federal–provincial sharing (Article 160).
However, provincial-to-district flows remain discretionary, often politically motivated.
Punjab's 2019 interim system and Sindh's ad hoc releases illustrate a vertical imbalance:
power concentrated at the province, responsibility pushed downward without money.

> Without fiscal autonomy, devolution is only a speech.

## 4. Administrative Power and Human Resources

Indonesia's districts gained authority to appoint, promote, and discipline civil servants within their territory (under the Civil Service Law 43/1999).
Local governments could tailor recruitment to sectoral needs — hiring midwives, teachers, or sanitation workers locally.

In Pakistan, district officers are still answerable upward to provincial secretariats.
The provincial cadre system (DMG/PMS) dominates; transfers are used to reward loyalty, not performance.
No local HR planning or training budget exists in most districts.

Result: demotivated staff, absenteeism, and a pervasive sense that "the district doesn't matter."

## 5. Planning, Data, and Accountability

Indonesia created *Bappeda* — Regional Development Planning Boards — in each district.
They prepare five-year plans (*RPJMD*) and annual budgets (*RKPD*) aligned with measurable outcomes, all open to public hearings (*musrenbang*).

Citizens can see how much is allocated to roads, clinics, or schools in their own area.

Pakistan's districts mostly operate without public planning forums. Annual Development Programs (ADPs) are prepared at the province; district plans are mere annexes, rarely discussed in councils.

The result: low transparency, weak alignment, and duplication.

**Example:**

A school built by a provincial department next to one built by a federal project — both without teachers.

### 6. Local Representation and Elections

Indonesia's local democracy is noisy but alive.
District heads and councils are elected every five years;
voter turnout regularly exceeds 70%.
This creates horizontal legitimacy — citizens can "punish" non-performing leaders through ballots.

Pakistan's local elections, by contrast, are sporadic and fragile.
The 2013–2018 period saw a five-year vacuum in many provinces.
When held, councils often lack fiscal authority or administrative teeth.

As a result, local governance remains ceremonial.
A councillor without budget is not a representative — he is a spectator.

## 7. District Performance: Comparative Indicators

| Indicator | Indonesia (2001→2023) | Pakistan (2010→2023) |
|---|---|---|
| % of national budget managed locally | 35% → 45% | 14% → 18% |

| | | |
|---|---|---|
| Literacy rate (avg across districts) | 67% → 95% | 52% → 63% |
| Infant mortality (per 1,000) | 46 → 21 | 74 → 59 |
| Local tax revenue share | 15% → 22% | 2% → 4% |
| Citizen satisfaction with local gov. | 60% → 81% | 38% → 46% |

(Data: World Bank WDI, Bappenas Indonesia, Pakistan Bureau of Statistics 2024)

## 8. Building District Compacts for Pakistan

The next phase of Pakistan's reform must not be another speech about "empowerment."
It requires legally binding district compacts, where each district signs a measurable agreement with its province — much like Indonesia's *performance-based transfers.*

## Each compact would include:

1. Basic service targets (literacy, immunization, safe water, maternal health).
2. Fiscal formula — automatic release tied to verified outcomes.
3. Citizen feedback loops — mobile apps, local assemblies, and annual public audits.
4. District transparency portals — publishing budgets, contracts, and procurement data.
5. Provincial oversight boards — staffed by civil society and retired auditors.

Such compacts shift politics from patronage to performance.

## 9. Institutional Tools and Safeguards

**To make local governance credible, three guardrails are essential:**

| Domain | Reform Instrument | Function |
|---|---|---|
| Fiscal Integrity | Provincial–District Fiscal Transparency Act | Mandates formula-based transfers, open data |
| Accountability | Independent District Audit Commission | Reviews accounts, hears citizen petitions |
| Civil Service | District Service Law | Creates local cadres, limits arbitrary transfers |

Together, they institutionalize what Indonesia achieved through practice: predictability + proximity + participation.


## 10. The Road to 2035 — Reclaiming Legitimacy

Pakistan's next decade must aim for a district revolution —
not of ideology, but of efficiency and respect.

**Targets (2025–2035):**

- Literacy: 85% nationwide, with every district above 70%.
- Infant mortality <25/1,000.
- 50% of public spending executed by districts.
- Citizen satisfaction ≥75%.

Annual progress should be published through District Scorecards, updated quarterly online.
Provinces meeting targets receive federal incentives; laggards face public exposure.

When citizens can see the state working in their own town,
they no longer need to be convinced of democracy —
they can feel it.

## 11. Conclusion: The Republic Returns Home

True sovereignty lives not in Islamabad's marble halls,
but in a functioning school in Kasur,
a clean street in Sukkur,
a maternity clinic in Swat.

Indonesia's lesson is that legitimacy is a local currency —
it must circulate daily or it expires.

For Pakistan, rebuilding from the district upward
means returning the republic to its rightful owners:
the citizens whose taxes, trust, and dignity sustain it.

## References (APA Style)

Buehler, M. (2010). *Decentralisation and Local Democracy in Indonesia.* Routledge.

Cheema, A., Khwaja, A., & Qadir, A. (2019). *Local Government Reforms in Pakistan: A Comparative Analysis.* Harvard Kennedy School.

Government of Indonesia. (2004). *Laws No. 32 and 33 on Regional Governance and Fiscal Balance.*

Government of Pakistan. (2010). *18th Constitutional Amendment.*

Shah, A. (2012). *Local Governance in Developing Countries.* World Bank.

Transparency International. (2023). *Subnational Governance Report.*

UNDP. (2024). *Human Development at the Local Level.*

World Bank. (2024). *World Development Indicators.*

# Chapter 9

## A Ten-Year Sprint (2026–2035): From Crisis Management to National Renewal

### 1. Abstract

Between 2026 and 2035, Pakistan faces its narrowest and last window for transformation.
The next decade must not be another cycle of crisis management — it must be a decade of recovery, reconstruction, and dignity.

Indonesia's first post-Suharto decade (1999–2009) turned collapse into resilience by combining macroeconomic stability with social investment and local empowerment.

**Pakistan can do the same if it commits to three core imperatives:**

1. Institutional discipline (no parallel budgets, no extra-constitutional centers of power).
2. Human capital acceleration (education, health, social protection).
3. Rule-of-law enforcement (from fiscal transparency to citizen equality).

The "Ten-Year Sprint" framework defines quantitative national targets, costed sectoral programs, and monitoring dashboards to be implemented jointly by federal, provincial, and district governments.

### 2. Why a Sprint, Not Another Plan

Pakistan has had dozens of "five-year plans" — yet no sustained ten-year discipline.

Each administration resets priorities; data resets too.
A sprint, unlike a plan, implies momentum, urgency, and completion.

The country's youth bulge (63% under age 30),
its growing urban middle class,
and the mounting pressure of debt and climate shocks
all demand a focused, time-limited strategy.

> "Development is not the multiplication of plans; it is the completion of promises."


## 3. Indonesia's Post-1998 Playbook: Lessons in Speed and Sequencing

**Between 1999–2009, Indonesia:**

- Cut poverty from 24% → 12%.
- Doubled per capita income ($900 → $1,800 nominal).
- Raised literacy to 95%, maternal mortality down by half.
- Restored fiscal discipline (deficit <2% GDP).

**Key drivers:**

- Fiscal rules: balanced budget, debt ceiling 60% GDP.
- Social investments: universal primary education, midwife-in-every-village program.
- Local governance: 40% of budget decentralized with public audits.
- Institutional memory: same development framework across three administrations.

The lesson: reforms succeed not when perfect, but when continuous.

## 4. Pakistan's Baseline (2025)

|  | 2025 Status | Target 2035 |
|---|---|---|
| GDP growth | 2.5% | ≥6% sustained |
| Public debt | 74% GDP | ≤60% |
| Literacy | 62% | ≥85% |
| Infant mortality | 57/1,000 | ≤25/1,000 |
| Female labor force participation | 22% | ≥40% |
| Corruption Perception Index | Score 28/100 | ≥55/100 |
| Export-to-GDP ratio | 10% | ≥20% |
| Renewable energy share | 4% | ≥20% |
| Trust in institutions (survey avg) | 35% | ≥70% |

These numbers define both urgency and possibility.

## 5. Strategic Axes of the Ten-Year Sprint

The "sprint" rests on five national axes, aligning governance, economy, and dignity.

| Axis | Goal | Key Mechanisms |
|---|---|---|
| ① Fiscal Discipline | End circular debt & hidden subsidies | Fiscal Responsibility Act, parliamentary oversight, provincial audits |
| ② Human Development | Educate, nourish, and protect every child | Education emergency fund, nutrition schemes, universal primary healthcare |
| ③ Industrial Diversification | Move from raw exports to value chains | Special Economic Corridors (Textile, Energy, Digital, Agro) |
| ④ Decentralized Governance | Empower districts, measure outcomes | District Compacts, Scorecards, citizen feedback apps |
| ⑤ Justice & Institutional Reform | Equality before law, enforcement integrity | Judicial reforms, police training, anti-corruption ombudsman |

## 6. Human Capital Acceleration

### Education:

- National Literacy Mission (2026–2030): mobilize 100,000 volunteer teachers.
- Convert ghost schools to community learning centers.
- Vocational institutes in every district linked to local industries.

### Health:

- Primary-care network expansion: 1,000 new Basic Health Units (BHUs) per year.
- Family planning integrated with women's economic empowerment.
- Telemedicine partnerships with provincial universities.

### Social Protection:

- Merge cash-transfer programs (BISP, Ehsaas) into *Unified Citizen Account* system.
- Biometric portability across provinces; link benefits to school attendance & vaccination.

These programs should consume no less than 6% of GDP collectively by 2030.

## 7. Economic Diversification and Green Growth

Pakistan's export base remains narrow: cotton, rice, leather, remittances. The Ten-Year Sprint must pivot toward "product complexity + green transition."

### Priority sectors:

1. Textile-to-technical unique
2. Agro-processing & cold-chain logistics.
3. Renewable manufacturing hubs (solar panels, EV components).

4.      Digital outsourcing & creative economy.

**Policy instruments:**

*       10-year tax stability for exporters investing in green technology.
*       Carbon-adjusted tariffs for domestic producers meeting emission targets.
*       "Made Local 25/10" initiative: 25% more domestic value-added in every export chain by 2035.

Indonesia's *downstreaming* strategy (nickel → EV batteries) shows that control over processing = sovereignty in trade.

## 8. Rule of Law and Institutional Integrity

**No sprint can succeed without trust.**
**Pakistan's legal architecture must therefore be cleaned and codified around three guarantees:**

1.      Budget transparency (open data for every department).
2.      Equal application of law (no military or political exemptions).
3.      Independent anti-corruption agency with prosecutorial power.

**Legal milestones:**

*       2026: Enact *Civil–Military Oversight Act* (based on Chapter 10 proposals).
*       2027: Establish *National Accountability Reform Commission*.
*       2028: Digitize all court filings and case tracking.
*       2030: Public release of *Annual Justice Index*.

## 9. Financing the Sprint

Estimated total cost (2026–2035):
≈ USD 210 billion, roughly 4% of GDP per year.

Funding mix:

- 50% reallocation from subsidies & inefficiencies.
- 30% concessional financing (ADB, WB, Islamic Dev. Bank).
- 10% diaspora bonds ("Invest in the Republic" initiative).
- 10% private co-investment (PPPs).

All spending under an independent *Fiscal Council* (modeled on Indonesia's BPK + Korea's Fiscal Policy Office).

Every rupee must be traceable through a public expenditure dashboard — accessible to journalists and citizens alike.


## 10. Monitoring and Public Participation

Governments tend to measure inputs, not outcomes.
The Ten-Year Sprint must flip that logic through public dashboards and citizen scoring.

| Tool | Function |
| --- | --- |
| District Scorecards | Track health, education, infrastructure outcomes quarterly |
| Citizen Audit Portals | Allow complaints and data verification |
| Annual "State of the Republic" Report | Published jointly by federal & provincial audit offices |
| Public Hearings in Parliament | Mandatory review of progress every March |

As Indonesia's *musrenbang* proved, participation breeds legitimacy — and legitimacy sustains growth.

## 11. The Spirit of the Sprint

A decade of sprinting is not about speed alone —
it is about discipline, dignity, and direction.

By 2035, Pakistan must emerge not as a "stabilized" country,
but as a self-respecting society —
one where a teacher is paid on time,
a patient is treated with care,
a soldier knows his lawful limits,
and a young citizen can dream without fear.

"The republic's success will not be written in GDP;
it will be written in the eyes of its people."

## 12. Key 2035 Milestones

| Domain | 2025 Baseline | 2035 Target | Lead Institution |
|---|---|---|---|
| Literacy | 62% | 85% | Ministry of Education + District Boards |
| Infant Mortality | 57/1,000 | ≤25/1,000 | Ministry of Health |
| Renewable Energy | 4% | 20% | Energy Commission |
| Export/GDP | 10% | 20% | Commerce & Industry Ministry |
| Public Debt | 74% GDP | ≤60% | Fiscal Council |
| Corruption Index | 28/100 | ≥55/100 | Anti-Corruption Commission |
| Citizen Trust | 35% | ≥70% | |

## 13. Conclusion: From Planning to Purpose

Plans fail when they belong to ministries;
they succeed when they belong to citizens.

Indonesia proved that a decade of disciplined action
can rewrite a nation's story.
Pakistan's "Ten-Year Sprint" can do the same —

if it starts not from IMF tables or elite meetings,
but from the district, the teacher, the patient, the worker,
and the citizen who believes change is possible.

This sprint is not a race against other nations;
it is a race back toward the republic itself.

## References (APA Style)

Asian Development Bank. (2024). *Pakistan Country Partnership Strategy 2024–2030.*
Bappenas Indonesia. (2012). *Indonesia's National Development Planning Post-Reformasi.*
Government of Pakistan. (2025). *Vision 2035 Policy Paper.*
IMF. (2024). *Pakistan Article IV Consultation Report.*
UNDP. (2024). *Human Development Index Database.*
World Bank. (2024). *World Development Indicators.*

# Chapter 10

## Constitutional Guardrails: Civilian Supremacy and the Duty to Refuse Unlawful Orders

### 1. Abstract

No democracy can survive without lawful boundaries on force.
From Latin America to Southeast Asia, nations that emerged from military dominance succeeded only when they rewrote the *rules of obedience*.

For Pakistan, this means not merely "civilian control" as a slogan,
but a constitutional redefinition of military duty itself —
a legal architecture where soldiers are *sworn to the Constitution and the people*, not to individuals or transient regimes.

This chapter proposes a full model article for Pakistan's Constitution, grounded in comparative law (Indonesia, Germany, South Africa, and Israel), linking civilian supremacy, lawful refusal, and institutional accountability.

### 2. The Core Idea: When Obedience Becomes a Crime

History's darkest moments — from Nuremberg to Dhaka — began when obedience replaced conscience.
Military and police orders, when detached from legality, mutate into state violence.
Therefore, every modern republic requires two levels of command:

      1.    Operational obedience — for lawful missions under civilian oversight.

      2.    Moral–legal disobedience — when orders violate the Constitution or international law.

This is not rebellion; it is the highest form of service.

"Obedience to the Constitution is the soldier's truest loyalty."
— *ButterflyMan, 2025*


## 3. Indonesia's Constitutional Evolution: From "Dwifungsi" to Civilian Rule

Under Suharto's New Order, the Indonesian Armed Forces (ABRI) embodied "Dwifungsi": dual roles in defense and governance.
They held parliamentary seats, ran businesses, and acted as local administrators.

### Reformasi (1998–2004) dismantled this system step by step:

- 1999: Military representation in parliament abolished (by 2004).
- 2000: Separation of police from military (TNI vs. POLRI).
- 2004: TNI Law 34 formalized "external defense only."
- 2005–2009: Internal security transferred to civil police; soldiers restricted to external missions.

### Result:

- Military budget under parliamentary oversight.
- Internal deployments required presidential decree + DPR (parliament) review.
- Inspector-General of the TNI created for internal accountability.

The *lesson for Pakistan*: depoliticization requires constitutional clarity, not verbal promises.

## 4. Pakistan's Civil–Military Imbalance: The Legal Blind Spot

Pakistan's Constitution (1973, as amended) asserts "civilian supremacy" in Article 243,
but in practice the chain of command remains extra-constitutional:

| Domain | Constitutional Provision | Operational Reality |
| --- | --- | --- |
| Armed Forces Command | Art. 243 – under federal government | De facto under GHQ, beyond civilian audit |
| Defense Budget | Subject to parliamentary approval | Classified; outside Auditor-General's mandate |
| Internal Deployment | Art. 245 – "in aid of civil power" | Invoked frequently without judicial review |
| Accountability | Military courts for soldiers | Overlapping with civilian jurisdiction; opaque |

Thus, constitutional silence breeds informal empire.
The corrective must be precise law, not moral expectation.


## 5. Legal Doctrine: The Concept of "Manifestly Unlawful Orders"

**The modern doctrine originates in:**

- Nuremberg Principle IV (1946): "Following orders" is no defense for crimes against humanity.
- German Soldiers Act (1956): Duty to refuse orders violating human dignity.
- Israeli Supreme Court (Kafr Qassem, 1957): "A black flag of illegality flies over such orders."
- South African Defence Act (1995): Soldiers must disobey manifestly unlawful orders and report them.

**These precedents define the test:**

Would a reasonable soldier recognize the order as illegal on its face?

If yes — refusal becomes duty, not defiance.

## 6. Proposed Constitutional Article for Pakistan

### Article X — Civilian Supremacy and Lawful Refusal of Unlawful Orders

1.  The Armed Forces exist to defend the State against external aggression and to fulfill duties expressly permitted by law.
Internal deployment shall occur only under conditions narrowly defined by statute, with parliamentary authorization and judicial review.

2.  No member of the Armed Forces shall obey an order that is manifestly unlawful, including orders to:

    - use force against peaceful assemblies,
    - conduct extra-judicial detention, torture, or collective punishment,
    - interfere with elections, courts, or the press.

3.  A member who, in good faith, refuses to execute a manifestly unlawful order shall not be criminally or disciplinarily liable. Whistleblower protections shall apply.

4.  Commanders issuing manifestly unlawful orders shall be subject to prosecution under military and civilian law.

5.  An independent Inspector-General for the Armed Forces and a Parliamentary Defense Committee shall oversee complaints, audits, and compliance.

6.  This Article shall be interpreted consistently with constitutional rights, international humanitarian law, and the principle established at Nuremberg that illegal orders create no duty of obedience.

## 7. Implementation Framework

### (a)  Legal Mechanisms

• Enact the Armed Forces Accountability Act (2026) to operationalize Article X.

• Amend the Army Act 1952, Air Force Act 1953, and Navy Ordinance 1961 to incorporate lawful refusal clauses.

• Define "manifestly unlawful" in legal terms through an interpretive annex.

### (b)  Institutional Mechanisms

• Create an Inspector-General (IGAF) with statutory independence and audit powers.

• Establish a Parliamentary Defense Oversight Committee (PDOC) with civilian members, retired judges, and veterans.

• Require all internal deployments to be gazetted and reviewed ex post by Parliament and the Supreme Court.

### (c)  Educational Mechanisms

• Integrate "Constitutional Ethics and Humanitarian Law" into military academies.

• Introduce annual *lawful-refusal drills* as part of officer training.

• Develop simulation exercises for commanders under civilian legal supervision.


## 8. Budgetary and Transparency Clauses

A republic's defense legitimacy lies not in secrecy but in accountability.
By 2030, all defense-related expenditures (excluding classified R&D) should be subject to the Public Accounts Committee and Auditor-General audit.

Suggested ratio:

- 90% of defense spending → publicly auditable.
- 10% (national security) → audited by a secure bipartisan subcommittee.

Indonesia, South Korea, and Chile achieved this balance —
proving that transparency strengthens, not weakens, national defense.


## 9. Emergency Powers and Judicial Safeguards

Reform of Article 245 ("aid of civil power") is vital.
New formulation should:

- Limit duration of internal deployments (e.g., 60 days renewable only by Parliament).
- Mandate judicial review of detentions within 48 hours.
- Require public notice specifying the geographic scope and objectives of deployment.

Emergency powers must expire automatically,
not perpetuate military involvement in civil governance.


## 10. The Moral and Strategic Rationale

Refusal of illegal orders is not defiance — it is the Republic's self-defense.
By constitutionalizing lawful refusal, Pakistan gains three things:

1. Moral credibility — both domestically and internationally.
2. Professionalization — aligning the Armed Forces with global norms.
3. Stability — ending cycles of coups and politicized interventions.

"The soldier who refuses to shoot at his people protects the nation's soul."
— *ButterflyMan, 2025*

# 11. Comparative Reference Table

| Country | Clause / Doctrine | Scope of Refusal | Oversight Mechanism |
|---|---|---|---|
| Germany | Soldiers Act (1956) | Human dignity clause | Parliamentary Commissioner for the Armed Forces |
| Israel | Kafr Qassem Doctrine | "Black flag" test | Military Advocate General |
| South Africa | Defence Act (1995) | Manifest illegality | Ombud + Parliamentary Committee |
| Indonesia | TNI Law 34/2004 | External defense only | DPR Commission I |
| Pakistan (Proposed) | Article X (2026) | Manifest illegality + external focus | IGAF + PDOC |

## 12. Anticipated Objections and Legal Responses

Objection 1: "This will weaken command discipline."
→ *Response:* Clear legal duty strengthens discipline by aligning obedience with law, not personality.

Objection 2: "It may encourage mutiny."
→ *Response:* Procedures (written objection → IGAF review → alternative assignment) prevent chaos.

Objection 3: "It will expose national secrets."
→ *Response:* Classified audits under secure bipartisan committees maintain secrecy within legality.

Objection 4: "Existing laws are sufficient."
→ *Response:* History disproves this — without constitutional clarity, parallel authority reemerges.

## 13. Proposed Timeline (2026–2030)

| Year | Reform Action | Lead Institution |
|---|---|---|
| 2026 | Enact Article X via constitutional amendment | Parliament of Pakistan |
| 2027 | Pass Armed Forces Accountability Act | Ministry of Defense + Law Division |
| 2028 | Establish IGAF & PDOC | National Assembly |
| 2029 | Integrate lawful refusal training into academies | Joint Staff HQ |
| 2030 | First annual Defense Transparency Report | Auditor-Genera |

## 14. Integration with International Law

### The doctrine aligns with:

- UN Code of Conduct for Law Enforcement Officials (1979)
- Geneva Conventions (1949)
- Rome Statute of the ICC (1998)
- International Covenant on Civil and Political Rights (1966)

These frameworks ensure that Pakistan's constitutional reforms are not Western impositions, but universal principles of humanity.

## 15. Conclusion: The Republic's Shield

Constitutions fail when they trust virtue instead of procedure.
Pakistan must now codify *how* loyalty is expressed —
not to rulers, but to the rule of law.

If this guardrail stands,
then a future officer facing an unlawful command
will have the courage to say,

"Sir, this order violates my oath."

That moment — calm, lawful, unarmed —

will mark Pakistan's true democratic rebirth.

"The power that refuses injustice becomes the Republic's conscience."
— *ButterflyMan, 2025*

## References (APA Style)

ButterflyMan. (2025). *The Future of Muslim Democracies.* 2510 Press.
Government of Indonesia. (2004). *TNI Law No. 34 on the Armed Forces.*
Government of Pakistan. (1973, amended 2010). *The Constitution of the Islamic Republic of Pakistan.*
Israeli Supreme Court. (1957). *Kafr Qassem Case.*
Nuremberg Tribunal. (1946). *Principles of International Law.*
South African Defence Act. (1995). *No. 42 of 1995.*
United Nations. (1979). *Code of Conduct for Law Enforcement Officials.*
World Bank. (2024). *Governance Indicators Dataset.*

# Chapter 11

## The Soldier's Oath and the Lawful Refusal: Restoring the Republic's Moral Compass

### 1. Abstract

The true strength of a republic lies not in the number of its weapons,
but in the conscience of those who hold them.

For Pakistan — like many post-colonial states — the military oath has long
been an instrument of obedience, not of law.
This chapter proposes a modern transformation of that oath:
from loyalty to personalities or offices,
to loyalty to the Constitution, human dignity, and lawful command.

Where Chapter 10 codified "civilian supremacy" in law,
Chapter 11 seeks to embed it in the mindset and training of every soldier.
It shows that lawful refusal, when institutionalized, becomes the foundation
of a professional, respected, and truly patriotic armed force.

### 2. The Oath as a Mirror of Power

Oaths are not ceremonial; they are political instruments.
They reveal who truly holds power and to whom it is accountable.

### Historical examples:

| Country | Pre-reform Oath | Post-reform Oath |
| --- | --- | --- |
| Germany (1944 → 1949) | "I swear loyalty to Adolf Hitler…" | "I swear to defend the Basic Law and the people." |
| Japan (1941 → 1947) | "Serve the Emperor, preserve the Empire." | "Serve the Constitution and the State." |
| Indonesia (1997 → 2004) | "Loyal to ABRI and Pancasila." | |

**In Pakistan, the Pakistan Army Act Oath (1952) reads:**

"I will bear true faith and allegiance to Pakistan and uphold the Constitution of the Islamic Republic of Pakistan."

But in practice, this oath has often been filtered through hierarchy, interpreted as loyalty to the chain of command rather than to the law.

The new vision requires restoring its original intent:
"allegiance to the Constitution" means allegiance to the people.

## 3. The Anatomy of a Modern Military Ethic

**A military's moral legitimacy rests on three pillars:**

| Pillar | Description | Example |
|---|---|---|
| 1. Lawful Obedience | Execute all lawful orders faithfully. | Respond to civilian chain of command. |
| 2. Lawful Refusal | Reject manifestly unlawful orders. | Refuse firing on unarmed civilians. |
| 3. Moral Courage | Act ethically even in ambiguity. | Protect life when legality is unclear. |

When only the first pillar exists, armies obey without thought.
When all three coexist, they become protectors of civilization.

"Discipline without conscience builds tyranny.
Conscience without discipline breeds chaos.
True professionalism balances both."
— *ButterflyMan, 2025*

## 4. Indonesia's Post-Reform Military Doctrine

**After 1998, Indonesia's TNI Doctrine of Sapta Marga was revised to include:**

1.    Service to the Republic and Constitution.

2.    Respect for human rights and humanitarian law.
3.    Obedience only to lawful orders.
4.    Loyalty to the people above any individual.

This doctrine, reinforced by training, ethics courses, and field drills,
helped rebuild the military's social legitimacy after decades of political
dominance.

By contrast, Pakistan's military still trains under a Cold War–era
command mentality,
where internal security justifies everything.
This must now evolve toward constitutional command culture.


## 5. The Proposed Modern Oath (Pakistan Armed Forces)

"I solemnly affirm that I will bear true faith and allegiance
to the Constitution of the Islamic Republic of Pakistan,
and uphold the dignity and rights of its people.
I shall defend Pakistan against external aggression
and obey all lawful orders issued under the Constitution and law.

I shall refuse any manifestly unlawful command,
and shall act in good faith to protect life, liberty, and justice.

May God be my witness and my judge in upholding this solemn oath."

This revised oath embodies both obedience and conscience,
linking service to the Republic's moral foundations.


## 6. Institutionalizing the Ethic

To ensure this oath becomes living practice,
three levels of institutionalization are essential:

## (a) Training Reform

- Introduce *"Law and Conscience"* module in all academies (PMAs, Air & Naval schools).
- Mandatory study of Pakistan's Constitution, Human Rights, and International Humanitarian Law.
- Scenario-based simulations: refusal of unlawful orders, civilian engagement, media ethics.

## (b) Command Culture

- Establish *Ethics Officer* roles at battalion and base level.
- Require every commanding officer to certify legality of written orders.
- Introduce *Anonymous Reporting Portals* within IGAF system.

## (d) Evaluation Metrics

- Annual "Ethical Conduct Index" for officers, scored by peers and subordinates.
- Public recognition of units showing excellence in lawful restraint during crises.
- Integration of lawful refusal into promotion criteria.

## 7. Lawful Refusal in Practice: The Chain of Responsibility

**A lawful refusal system must balance ethics with discipline.**

**Procedure:**

1. Immediate Written Objection: Officer/soldier records reasons for believing an order is unlawful.
2. Review by Legal Advisor / IGAF: Rapid 24-hour review; if confirmed unlawful → alternative assignment.
3. Protection Clause: Refusing officer shielded from retaliation; disciplinary immunity guaranteed.

4.   Command Liability: If order later found unlawful, issuing commander faces investigation.

**This process transforms refusal from chaos into regulated integrity.**


## 8. Case Studies: When Refusal Saved Nations

- Germany 1944: A few officers refused mass execution orders — post-war, they were declared national heroes.
- Indonesia 1998: Units that refused to fire on students became symbols of democratic loyalty.
- Tunisia 2011: The army's refusal to crush protests preserved the republic.
- Pakistan (future vision): Soldiers who choose law over command will become founders of a lawful defense culture.

"History will not remember those who obeyed without thought;
it will remember those who thought before obeying."
— *ButterflyMan, 2025*


## 9. Linking Military Ethics to National Renewal

Lawful refusal is not an isolated military doctrine —
it's the moral foundation of the entire state apparatus.
When the armed forces internalize legality,
police, bureaucracy, and local governance follow.

Indonesia's example proved this domino effect:
the moment the army stopped suppressing civilians,
citizens began to trust the state again.
Taxes rose, corruption fell, and investment confidence returned.

Pakistan's future requires the same pivot:
from *"Fear of Power"* → *"Trust in Law."*

## 10. Integration with Religious and Cultural Values

Islamic tradition supports justice over blind obedience:

- Qur'an 4:135:
"O you who believe! Stand out firmly for justice,
even against yourselves, your parents, or your kin."
- Hadith (Sahih Muslim 1840):
"There is no obedience to the creation in disobedience to the Creator."

Thus, lawful refusal aligns religious faith with constitutional duty.
A soldier refusing to harm innocents acts in both legal and spiritual righteousness.


## 11. Legal Safeguards and Accountability

**For lawful refusal to work without chaos:**

1. IGAF must issue **Annual Compliance Reports to Parliament.**
2. Civil courts retain final review authority over "manifest illegality."
3. Commanders must maintain written records of all orders involving domestic deployment.
4. Military schools must publish annual syllabi for public transparency.

Such measures ensure that conscience operates within structure — not outside it.


## 12. The Cultural Shift: From "Power" to "Honor"

For seventy years, Pakistani soldiers have been taught that "discipline" equals "silence."
The new doctrine must teach that discipline equals lawful duty.
Honor lies not in fear or obedience, but in integrity.

Training films, public messaging, and national days (e.g. *Constitution Day*) should celebrate stories of soldiers who protected citizens rather than persecuted them.

This redefines heroism —
from domination to defense, from control to conscience.


## 13. Implementation Timeline (2026–2035)

| Year | Reform Measure | Lead Institution |
|------|----------------|------------------|
| 2026 | Official adoption of Revised Oath | Ministry of Defence + Parliament |
| 2027 | Establish Military Ethics Department | Joint Staff HQ |
| 2028 | Launch "Law and Conscience" curriculum | PMA / Air / Naval Academies |
| 2029 | IGAF portal for lawful refusal cases | IGAF Office |
| 2030 | First Ethical Conduct Index report | PDOC + National Audit Office |
| 2031–35 | Public awareness + commemorations | Ministry of Information |

## 14. Expected Outcomes

**By 2035:**

• Every soldier swears an oath to *the Constitution, not to commanders.*
• Refusal of unlawful orders is seen as *honor, not disobedience.*
• The military becomes *a national institution, not a parallel state.*
• Civil–military harmony replaces suspicion.
• Pakistan becomes a case study in Muslim-world democratization.

## 15. Conclusion: Conscience as Command

When law and morality converge,
obedience becomes sacred.

When they diverge,
obedience becomes sin.

The reformed soldier's oath transforms this moral paradox into a guiding light.
It aligns Pakistan's defense forces with the republic's spirit —
a spirit rooted in law, faith, and humanity.

> "The soldier's greatest victory is not defeating enemies,
> but refusing injustice."
> — *ButterflyMan, 2025*

## References (APA Style)

ButterflyMan. (2025). *The Future of Muslim Democracies.* 2510 Press.
Government of Pakistan. (1952). *Pakistan Army Act (and Oath of Allegiance).*
Government of Indonesia. (2004). *TNI Law No. 34 on the Armed Forces.*
Japan Constitution. (1947). *Article 66: Civilian Control of the Military.*
Nuremberg Tribunal. (1946). *Principles of International Law.*
Qur'an. (Surah An-Nisa, 4:135).*
Sahih Muslim. (Hadith 1840).*
UNESCO. (2024). *Military Ethics Education: Comparative Review.*

# Chapter 12

## Redefining National Security: From Moral Defense to Civilizational Defense

### 1. Abstract

National security is not the absence of war;
it is the presence of justice.

For Pakistan, the 21st century offers a paradox:
it spends billions defending borders,
yet remains vulnerable inside —
to poverty, disinformation, corruption, and internal mistrust.

This chapter proposes a new doctrine of security
rooted in constitutional ethics, civic participation, and regional cooperation
—
a transformation from power-based defense to value-based defense,
from guns to governance.

### 2. The Old Paradigm: Security as Control

Since 1947, Pakistan's security has been defined in negative terms —
what to fear, what to suppress, what to defend against.

- The army was tasked with defending both the borders *and* the idea of the state.
- Internal dissent was equated with external conspiracy.
- Budgets grew, but institutions stagnated.
- The result: citizens became *subjects*, not *stakeholders*.

By 2025, Pakistan's defense spending equals 3.8% of GDP,
while education and health combined barely reach 3.1%.
This imbalance is not strength — it is systemic fragility.

Security built on fear breeds dependency;
security built on dignity creates peace.

## 3. Indonesia's Shift: From Regime Survival to Public Security

Post-1998, Indonesia rewrote its defense white paper around one phrase:

"Security belongs to the people, not the rulers."

## Key transformations included:

| Reform Area | Before 1998 | After 2004 |
|---|---|---|
| Doctrine | "Regime security" (internal suppression) | "People's security" (external defense only) |
| Budget Oversight | Military-controlled | Parliamentary committees |
| Deployment | Internal policing allowed | Internal deployment only by law + court review |
| Civic Link | Minimal | Annual civilian–military dialogues |
| Transparency | Classified | Budget and procurement open to audit |

The result:
Indonesia reduced military business holdings (*Milbus*) by 80%, stabilized its politics, and improved global trust rankings.

Security was no longer a tool of fear — it became a public service.

## 4. Pakistan's Current Dilemma

**Pakistan's security establishment remains trapped in two competing logics:**

1. **Institutional Self-Preservation:**
The system prioritizes internal control over public trust.

2. **Moral Erosion:**

When corruption or torture becomes normalized,
the "protector" loses legitimacy.

Internal security laws (e.g., Anti-Terrorism Act, 1997; PECA, 2016)
often exceed proportional necessity — criminalizing speech instead of
violence.

The challenge ahead is not military defeat,
but ethical realignment.
When power outgrows accountability,
the republic shrinks.


## 5. A New Security Doctrine (Five Axes)

The future of defense must be defined not by weapons,
but by values, competence, and trust.

| Axis | Vision | Instruments |
|---|---|---|
| ① Constitutional Defense | Protect law above all else | Legal refusal doctrine (Ch.10–11), parliamentary oversight |
| ② Human Security | Education, food, health as defense pillars | 10-Year Sprint targets integrated into defense planning |
| ③ Digital & Cognitive Defense | Fight misinformation with civic literacy | Media education, digital ethics curriculum |
| ④ Regional Cooperation | Security through interdependence | South Asia–ASEAN peace corridor, joint disaster drills |
| ⑤ Ecological Defense | Protect land and water as sovereignty assets | Climate resilience fund, river protection laws |

This structure expands "national defense"
to include citizens' well-being as the first line of security.


## 6. Human Security as the Core of Defense

Amartya Sen and Mahbub ul Haq (1994) defined human security as:

"Freedom from fear, freedom from want, and freedom to live in dignity."

For Pakistan, this must translate into:

• Food Security: end malnutrition through district-based grain reserves.
• Health Security: universal primary healthcare as a constitutional right.
• Education Security: protect every child's access to schooling, even in conflict zones.
• Gender Security: ensure protection of women and minorities from violence.

A soldier defending borders while citizens die of hunger
is a contradiction in terms.
True patriotism begins where people no longer need to fear their own government.

## 7. The Role of the Soldier in a Constitutional Republic

The modern soldier must embody three loyalties:

1. To the Constitution — not to a person or party.
2. To Human Dignity — never to humiliate the powerless.
3. To Professional Honor — obedience within the limits of law.

When this triad replaces political loyalty,
discipline becomes moral strength.

Indonesia's "Law No. 34/2004" offers a model:

"The TNI (armed forces) shall maintain neutrality in political life and uphold human rights as the essence of service."

Pakistan can codify a similar clause in its Defense Act revision (2030 target).

## 8. Economic and Civic Dimensions of Security

A nation that cannot manage its economy
cannot sustain its army.

By integrating economic resilience into defense policy,
Pakistan can stabilize without endless foreign debt.

## Key proposals:

- Create a Defense–Development Council to align industrial and defense innovation.
- Invest in local production of renewable energy to reduce import dependency.
- Introduce "Service Year Program" — one year of national or civic service for youth (civil + defense).
- Promote defense diplomacy: joint climate response, cyber cooperation, peacekeeping.

Thus, the defense sector becomes a source of innovation, not isolation.


## 9. Reframing Internal Security: From Surveillance to Trust

No democracy can survive if citizens feel watched but not protected.

**Pakistan's internal security architecture must evolve toward community-based policing, mediation, and social intelligence rather than mass surveillance.**

- End arbitrary detention under "national security" justifications.
- Shift resources from intelligence expansion to citizen engagement.
- Develop a "National Resilience Curriculum" in schools — teaching critical thinking, ethics, and coexistence.

Security begins not in barracks,
but in classrooms and courtrooms.

## 10. Regional Peace Architecture

Lasting peace requires shared institutions, not just treaties.

Drawing from ASEAN's post-1998 peace framework, Pakistan should pursue:

| Initiative | Partner | Purpose |
|---|---|---|
| SAARC–ASEAN Dialogue Forum | Indonesia, Bangladesh, Malaysia | Joint policy exchange on decentralization and military ethics |
| South Asia Disaster Corps | Sri Lanka, Nepal | Joint rescue and climate operations |
| Trade-for-Peace Corridors | India (under WTO facilitation) | Economic interdependence reducing hostility |
| Islamabad–Jakarta Peace Institute | Academic partnership | Research on constitutional reform and pluralism |

The purpose is not idealism, but pragmatic coexistence —
as Indonesia's President Yudhoyono once said:

**"Peace is not weakness; it is the highest form of intelligence."**

## 11. Ethical Defense Education (2026–2035)

A transformation in doctrine requires transformation in education.

**Proposed milestone**

| Year | Reform | Responsible Body |
|---|---|---|
| 2026 | Integrate "Human Security" into defense syllabus | National Defense University |
| 2027 | Joint civil–military ethics workshops | Ministry of Defense + UNDP |
| 2028 | Establish National Peace Leadership Academy | Islamabad |
| 2029 | Introduce "Service Year Program" pilot | Federal Youth Council |
| 2030 | Defense Act Amendment: Civilian Oversight Clause | Parliament |

| 2032– 2035 | Annual Peace and Security Dialogues | Regional partners |
|---|---|---|

By 2035, security education must teach ethics, empathy, and ecology — the new three "E's" of defense.

## 12. The Moral Equation of Power

Power without purpose destroys.
Purpose without law collapses.

The republic's safety depends on uniting both —
discipline guided by conscience,
and conscience protected by law.

This is the meaning of "moral defense."

It does not mean weakness or pacifism;
it means power under moral authority.
A soldier who refuses an unjust order defends the nation more deeply
than one who blindly obeys.

## 13. Civilizational Defense: The Next Frontier

A civilization survives not by its armies,
but by the values it refuses to betray.

Civilizational defense means protecting:

- Truth from propaganda,
- Compassion from hatred,
- Justice from corruption,
- Memory from erasure.

For Muslim democracies,
this doctrine bridges faith and freedom.

Islam's concept of *adl* (justice) and *amanah* (trust)
align perfectly with the constitutional ethos of equality and responsibility.

Pakistan can thus pioneer a model of ethical security
that inspires the Muslim world toward peace through dignity.

## 14. Indicators of Transformation (2035 Targets)

| Domain | Indicator | 2025 Baseline | 2035 Goal |
|---|---|---|---|
| Defense Accountability | Annual audit reports published | 1/5 | 5/5 |
| Public Trust in Military | Gallup score | 35% | ≥70% |
| Human Security Index | UNDP composite | 0.56 | ≥0.75 |
| Regional Peace Index | Economist Intelligence Unit | 2.1 | ≤1.5 |
| Defense–Development Ratio | Defense/Education+Health | 1.3 : 1 | 0.8 : 1 |

**These are not symbolic metrics —
they are the anatomy of national dignity.**

## 15. Conclusion: From Sword to Covenant

The republic's survival will not depend on new missiles,
but on new moral compasses.

If Pakistan can align power with principle —
as Indonesia began to do after 1998 —
it can finally move from perpetual insecurity
to a mature, law-bound peace.

"A nation is secure not when it is feared,
but when it is trusted."
— *ButterflyMan, 2025*

This is the ultimate defense —
the defense of civilization itself.


## References (APA Style)

Amartya Sen & Mahbub ul Haq. (1994). *Human Development Report: New Dimensions of Security.* UNDP.
Asian Development Bank. (2024). *Pakistan Governance and Resilience Report.*
ButterflyMan. (2025). *The Future of Muslim Democracies.* 2510 Press.
Government of Indonesia. (2004). *Defense Law No. 3/2004.*
Government of Pakistan. (2025). *National Security Policy Framework.*
UNDP. (2024). *Human Security Index.*
World Bank. (2024). *South Asia Peace and Development Dashboard.*